Word
MADE EASY

A beginner's guide including how-to skills and projects

Ewan Arthur

ARCTURUS

This edition published in 2013 by Arcturus Publishing Limited
26/27 Bickels Yard, 151–153 Bermondsey Street,
London SE1 3HA

Microsoft product screen shots reprinted with permission from Microsoft Corporation.

Microsoft, Word, Excel, and Windows Vista are trademarks of the Microsoft group of companies.

Excel Made Easy is an independent publication and is not affiliated with, nor has it been authorized, sponsored, or otherwise approved by Microsoft Corporation.

The materials in this book relate to Microsoft Office 2010.

Prepared for Arcturus by Starfish Design Editorial and Project Management Ltd.

ISBN: 978-1-84858-418-1
AD001921US

Printed in China

Contents

How to use this book

This book will help you learn how to use Microsoft **Word**, probably the most popular word processor in the world.

- It is written for beginners and covers only what you really need.

- There's no jargon, just simple instructions and lots of pictures. You'll start with the basics and soon be able to write letters, design posters and add pictures.

- Every left hand page is called *How to do it* and teaches a new skill. Every right hand page is called *Using it* and has a fun exercise to practice that skill.

HOW TO DO IT

This explains each skill and the steps needed to use the skill. Pictures show you what's on your computer screen.

USING IT

These exercises make up a series of projects. The *Using it* pages also have simple step-by-step stages with pictures.

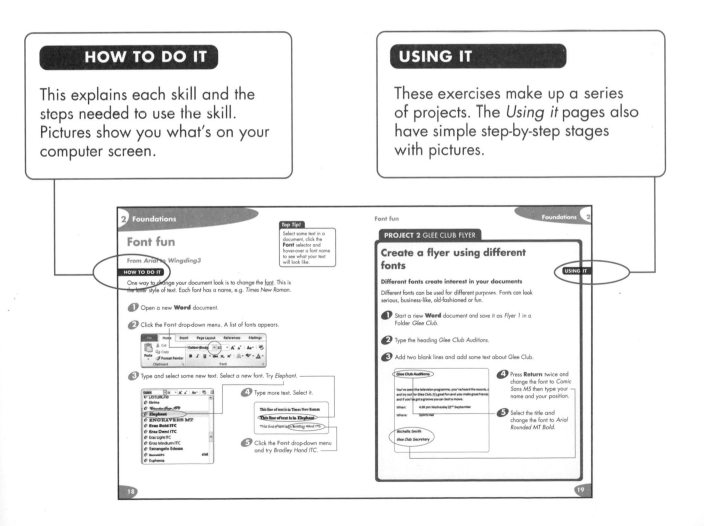

The Microsoft Office **Word** window

What you will see when you open **Word**:

The **Quick Access Toolbar** – does most of the very common tasks such as Open and Save, but without any options.

The **Ribbon** – is where most of the options that you will learn about are found.

The **Horizontal Ruler** – shows you the text edges at the sides of the document.

The **Close** button. Click to exit **Word**.

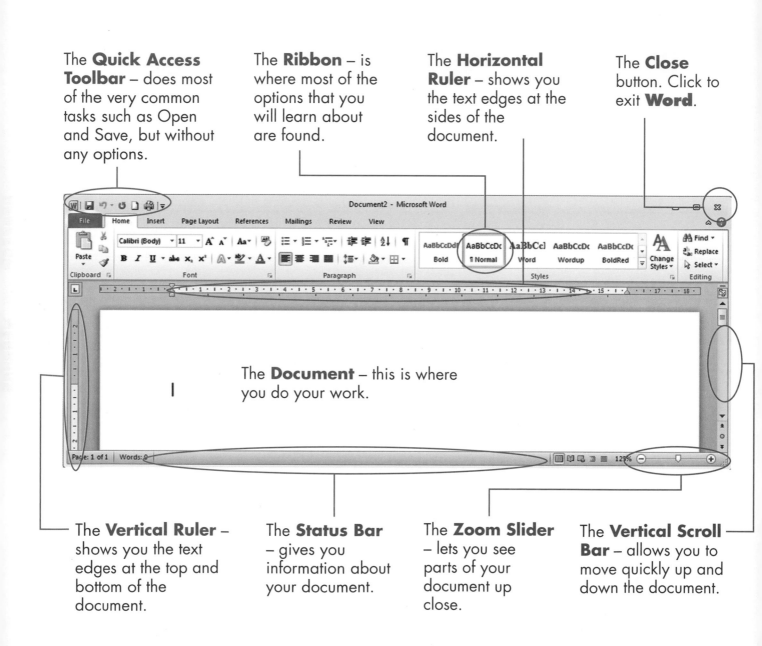

The **Document** – this is where you do your work.

The **Vertical Ruler** – shows you the text edges at the top and bottom of the document.

The **Status Bar** – gives you information about your document.

The **Zoom Slider** – lets you see parts of your document up close.

The **Vertical Scroll Bar** – allows you to move quickly up and down the document.

The ribbon

The **ribbon** is where to find most of the tools you use. The ribbon is divided into **tabs**. Each tab is split up into sets of tools. **Word** is clever and, depending on what you are doing, puts useful tabs in the ribbon.

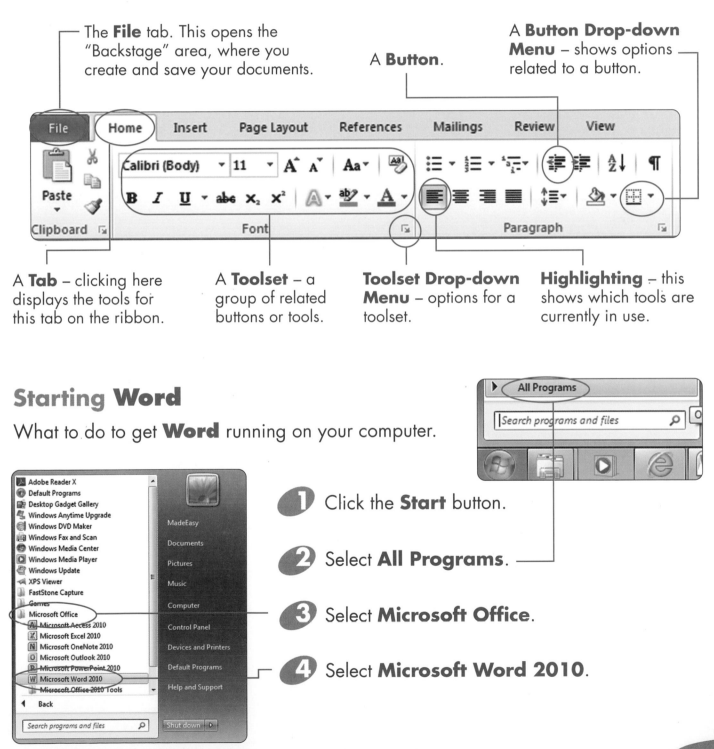

The **File** tab. This opens the "Backstage" area, where you create and save your documents.

A **Button**.

A **Button Drop-down Menu** – shows options related to a button.

A **Tab** – clicking here displays the tools for this tab on the ribbon.

A **Toolset** – a group of related buttons or tools.

Toolset Drop-down Menu – options for a toolset.

Highlighting – this shows which tools are currently in use.

Starting **Word**

What to do to get **Word** running on your computer.

1 Click the **Start** button.

2 Select **All Programs**.

3 Select **Microsoft Office**.

4 Select **Microsoft Word 2010**.

Using the mouse

You will use a mouse and keyboard with **Word**. You can often use either to do the same thing. For example, get help by pressing the **F1** function key or clicking on the ⑦ icon.

Common terms and techniques

Right-click – press and release the <u>right</u>-hand button.

Click – press and release the <u>left</u>-hand button.
Two quick clicks is a **Double-Click**.

Click-and-drag – press the left mouse button, move (or drag) the cursor, then release it. This either highlights everything covered or moves whatever was selected by the first click.

Mouse pointer – moving the mouse moves the mouse pointer around the screen. It changes depending on what is going on.

Hover-over – keep the mouse pointer over a button for a few seconds. This will often produce a pop-up message.

Cursor – the flashing line (cursor) shows where type will appear when entered.

Using the keyboard

Common terms and techniques

Esc – closes any pop-up windows you don't want any more.

Caps Lock – when pressed, everything is typed in capital letters.

Function keys – can be used as shortcuts for tools and options. The **F7** key starts the spelling checker.

Backspace – deletes text to the <u>left</u> of the cursor.

Delete – deletes text to the <u>right</u> of the cursor.

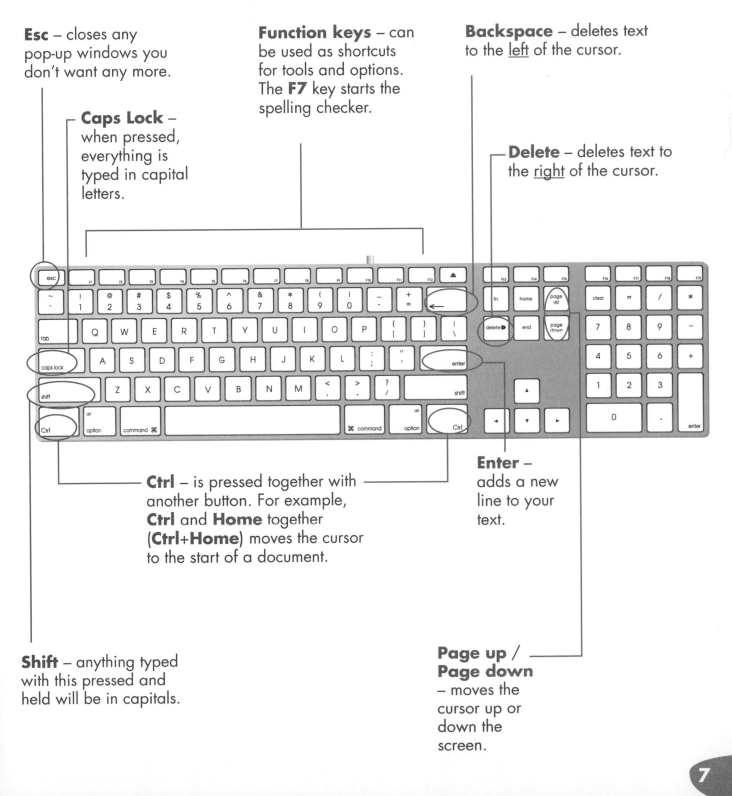

Ctrl – is pressed together with another button. For example, **Ctrl** and **Home** together (**Ctrl+Home**) moves the cursor to the start of a document.

Enter – adds a new line to your text.

Shift – anything typed with this pressed and held will be in capitals.

Page up / Page down – moves the cursor up or down the screen.

Launching Word

Creating and **Saving** documents

Top Tip!

This can be done from the "Quick Access" toolbar. Click the **New** and **Save** buttons.

Start a new document and save it so you can use it again.

1 Click on the **File** tab on the left of the **ribbon**.

2 From the options that open on the left of the screen, click on **New**.

3 The "Backstage" area shows many document types. Double-click on **Blank document**.

4 A new document will open. Type your address in it.

5 To save your document, click on the **File** tab and then on **Save**.

6 The "Save As" dialog box opens. Type *My Address* in the "File name" field. Then click **Save**.

Remember!

Word opens with a new document automatically.

PROJECT 1 FIRST STEPS

Your first Word

Create a new Word document and save it

USING IT

A gentle introduction to using **Word**.

 Open a new document.

 Type your name.

 Press the **Enter** key twice.

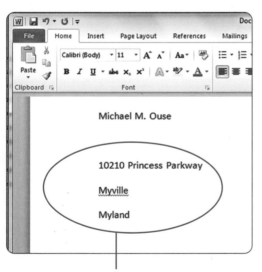

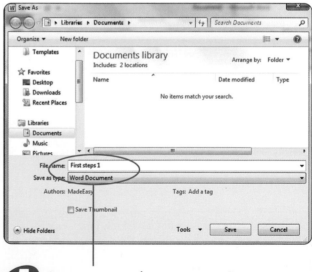

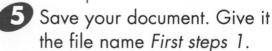 Type your address. Press **Enter** and add your country.

5 Save your document. Give it the file name *First steps 1*.

6 Close **Word** by clicking on the **Close** button at the top right corner of the screen.

Opening existing documents and using folders

Open your documents and organize where you save them

When you create a lot of documents it's good to organize them and keep copies as back up.

Top Tip!

Make important files easy to find by clicking on the pin next to the file name in the recent list.

First steps 1
My Documents

1 Open **Word** again, then click on the **File** tab.

2 The "Backstage" area opens to **Recent Documents**. Double-click on the file you want to open.

3 If the document is not in the recent list, click on the **Open** button.

4 The "Open" dialog box pops up allowing you to find your file on your computer.

5 To save a copy of the document, click on the **Save As** button in the **File** tab.

6 You can save it with a new name and/or save it in another folder. Folders allow you to organize your files. Use the **New Folder** button in the dialog box to create new folders.

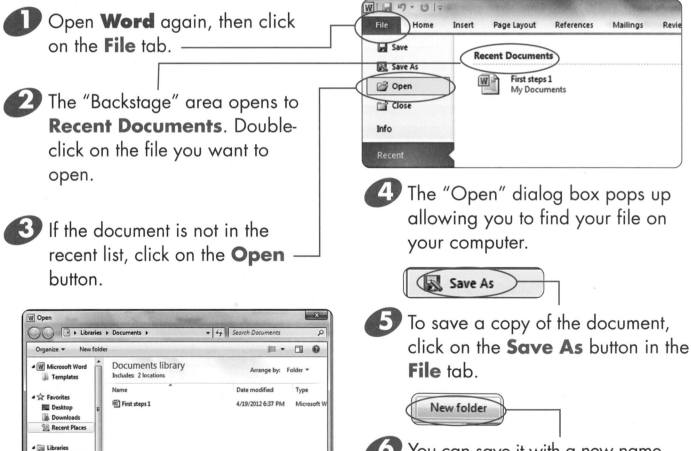

PROJECT 1 FIRST STEPS

Retrieve your saved document and copy it to a new folder

Open *First steps 1* and save it in a new folder as *First steps 2*

Create a back up of your document in a folder where you will find it easily.

 Open **Word** and then click on the **File** tab.

 Open your *First steps 1* document, either from the recent list or the "Open" dialog box.

3 Click on the **File** tab and then **Save As**.

4 Click on the **New Folder** button. A new folder appears in the dialog box and you can type in the name *First steps*, then press **Enter**.

5 Double-click on your new folder and rename your document *First steps 2*.

6 Close **Word** again.

Saving to the cloud

Make your work available online

HOW TO DO IT

Word allows you to save your work to the internet so that you can access it from anywhere.

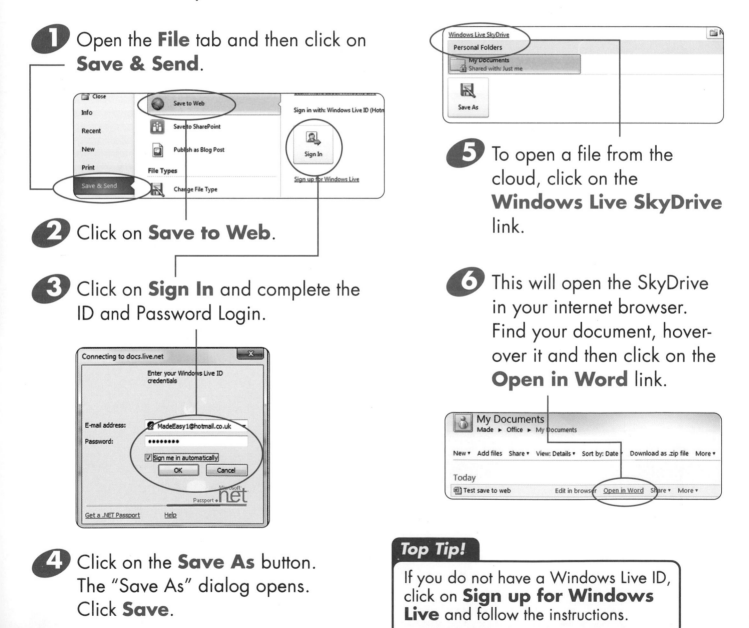

1 Open the **File** tab and then click on **Save & Send**.

2 Click on **Save to Web**.

3 Click on **Sign In** and complete the ID and Password Login.

4 Click on the **Save As** button. The "Save As" dialog opens. Click **Save**.

5 To open a file from the cloud, click on the **Windows Live SkyDrive** link.

6 This will open the SkyDrive in your internet browser. Find your document, hover-over it and then click on the **Open in Word** link.

Top Tip!

If you do not have a Windows Live ID, click on **Sign up for Windows Live** and follow the instructions.

PROJECT 1 FIRST STEPS

Save your *First steps* 2 to the cloud

You will be able to access this document anywhere

Use the cloud to store your document and open it again.

1 Open your *First steps 2* document.

2 Sign in to Windows Live.

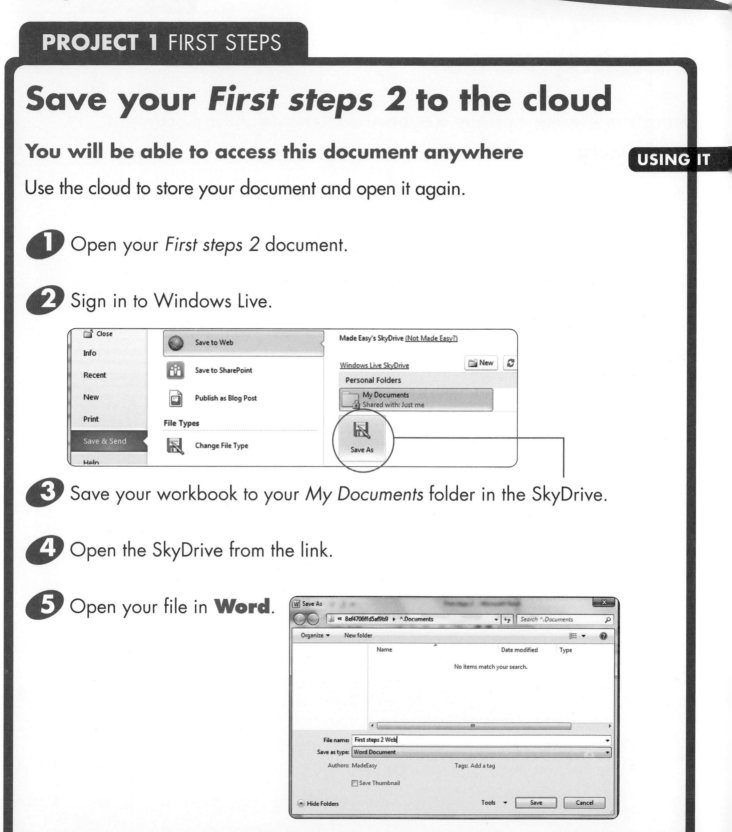

3 Save your workbook to your *My Documents* folder in the SkyDrive.

4 Open the SkyDrive from the link.

5 Open your file in **Word**.

Getting about

Using the **Mouse** and the **Keyboard** to create your document

HOW TO DO IT

Using the mouse or the keyboard, you can add, change or delete any part of your document.

> This is where the cursor is |but it should be flashing

1 To add text to a different part of the document, move the mouse pointer and click or use the **Arrow** keys.

> This is where the mouse pointer is when it is over the I text area

2 If you can't see the part where you want to type, click-and-drag the "Scroll Bar" or use the **Page Up** and **Page Down** keys.

3 Use the **Backspace** key to delete text to the left of the cursor, or the **Delete** key to delete text to the right.

> This is a block of text that has been selected by using click-and-drag

4 To delete a lot of text, click-and-drag the mouse pointer across the text, then press the **Delete** key.

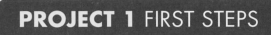

PROJECT 1 FIRST STEPS

Add to and delete from *First steps 2*

Change the information shown in the document

USING IT

The second version of *First steps* can now be changed.

 Open *First steps 2*.

> Michael M. Ouse
>
> |
>
> 10210 Princess Parkway

2 Click on the blank line after your name and add your date of birth.

> Michael M. Ouse
>
> November 28th 1928|

3 Select your country by using click-and-drag.

4 Press the **Backspace** key to delete the *country* and press it again to get the cursor up to the end of your address.

5 Save your document.

Top Tip!

Add the **Open** button to your "Quick Access" menu. Click on the drop-down menu and select "Open."

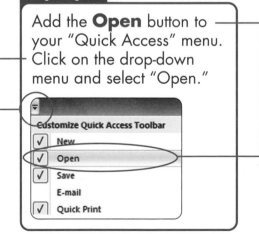

Can you see what it is yet?

It is easier to navigate and read your document if it's at the correct Zoom setting

The default zoom is 100% – **Word** is showing you what your document would look like if printed. But you might want to make it bigger for more detail or smaller for an overview.

Remember!

There are many more options in the **View** tab. Take time to explore them.

 Click the **View** tab. ————

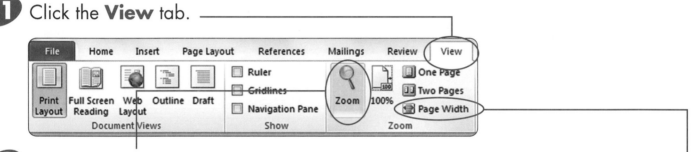

2 Click the **Zoom** button. The "Zoom" dialog box appears.

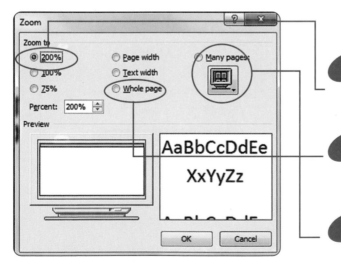

3 To make the document really big, select *200%* then click **OK**.

4 To fit the whole page onto your screen, select *Whole page*.

5 To see several pages at once, select the *Many pages* option.

Top Tip!

Look at the "Status Bar." The "Zoom Slider" is for quickly zooming in and out.

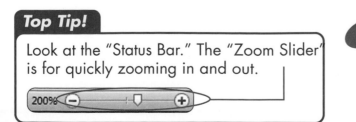

6 To make the document fit the screen width, click the **View** tab then the **Page Width** button. —

Find the perfect setting for you and your screen

Adjust the zoom so that you can see as much of your document as you need

Let's add to the document and see what we can see.

 Open *First steps 1*.

 Move the cursor to the end and then press **Enter** until a new page has started.

3 Type *Yours faithfully* and your name.

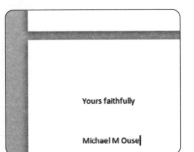

4 Use the "Many pages" option in the "Zoom" dialog box to see both pages.

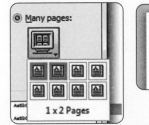

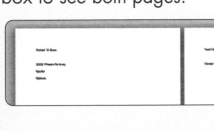

 Use the **Page Width** button to make the document fill the screen.

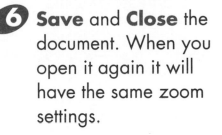

6 **Save** and **Close** the document. When you open it again it will have the same zoom settings.

Top Tip!

Select some text in a document, click the **Font** selector and hover-over a font name to see what your text will look like.

Font fun

From *Arial* to *Wingding3*

HOW TO DO IT

One way to change your document look is to change the <u>font</u>. This is the letter style of text. Each font has a name, e.g. *Times New Roman*.

1 Open a new **Word** document.

2 Click the **Font** drop-down menu. A list of fonts appears.

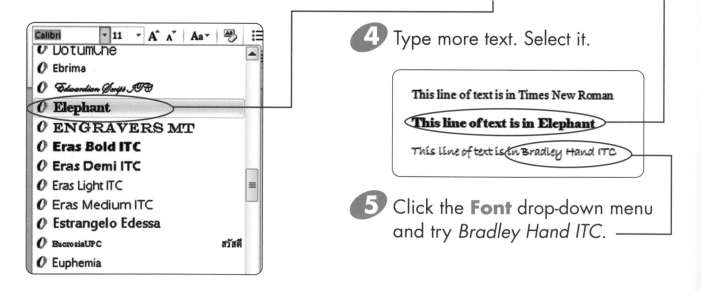

3 Type and select some new text. Select a new font. Try *Elephant*. —

4 Type more text. Select it.

This line of text is in Times New Roman

This line of text is in Elephant

This line of text is in Bradley Hand ITC

5 Click the **Font** drop-down menu and try *Bradley Hand ITC*. —

PROJECT 2 GLEE CLUB FLYER

Create a flyer using different fonts

USING IT

Different fonts create interest in your documents

Different fonts can be used for different purposes. Fonts can look serious, business-like, old-fashioned or fun.

 Start a new **Word** document and save it as *Flyer 1* in a Folder *Glee Club*.

 Type the heading *Glee Club Auditions*.

❸ Add two blank lines and add some text about Glee Club.

Glee Club Auditions

You've seen the television program, you've heard the records, now It's great fun and you make great friends. So come along and sing y groove you can bust a move.

When: 4.00 pm Wednesday September 22nd

Where: Sports Hall

Michelle Smith

Glee Club Secretary

❹ Press **Enter** twice and change the font to *Comic Sans MS* then type your name and your position.

❺ Select the title and change the font to *Arial Rounded MT Bold*.

Size matters

Top Tip!

Use the **Clear Formatting** button to go back to the font you had before.

Font sizes 1–72

HOW TO DO IT

Big letters make an impact. Small letters are harder to read but allow room for more information.

1 Open a **Word** document. On the **Home** tab click the **Grow Font** button. Start typing. Clicking the **Grow Font** button again makes the text even bigger.

2 Now shrink your text using the **Shrink Font** button.

3 Select some text and choose a new size from the **Font Size** button drop-down menu. Hover-over over a size to preview how it looks.

4 You can also type a size directly into the **Font Size** button field.

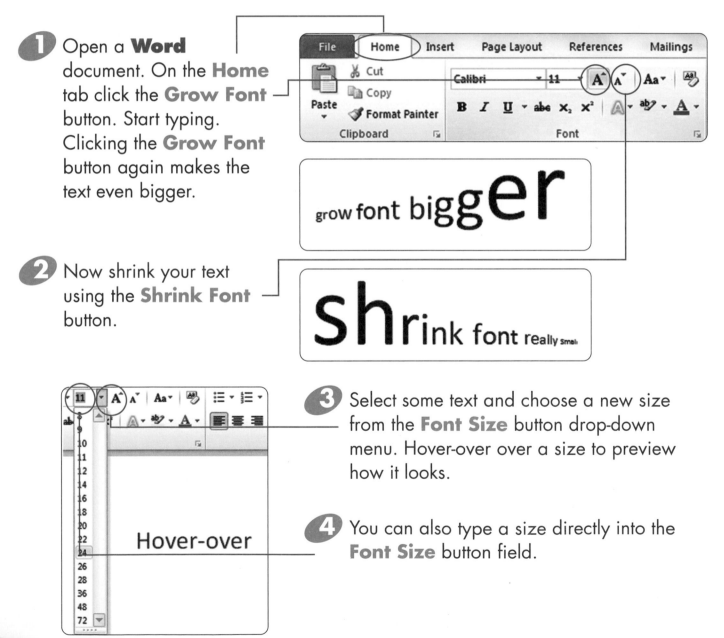

PROJECT 2 GLEE CLUB FLYER

Change the title font size

Make your flyer title really big

Most posters and flyers have a big title and usually some small print too.

1 Select your flyer's title and select 36 point from the drop-down menu.

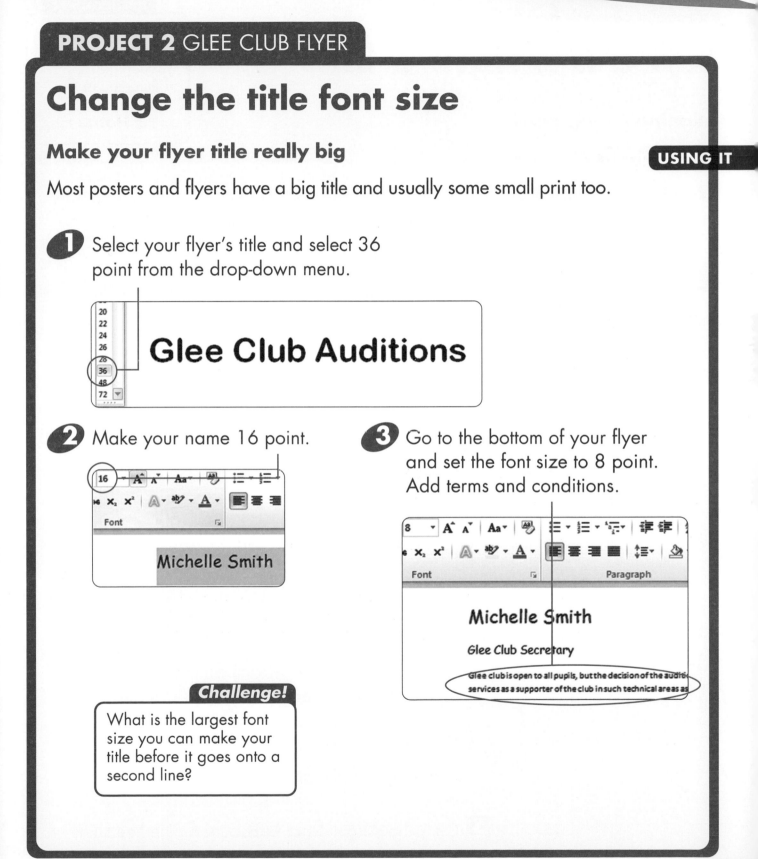

Glee Club Auditions

2 Make your name 16 point.

Michelle Smith

3 Go to the bottom of your flyer and set the font size to 8 point. Add terms and conditions.

Michelle Smith

Glee Club Secretary

Glee club is open to all pupils, but the decision of the auditi...
services as a supporter of the club in such technical areas as...

Challenge!

What is the largest font size you can make your title before it goes onto a second line?

Left a bit, right a bit

Aligning paragraphs

Remember!

The alignment of the text you are working on is highlighted in the "Paragraph" toolset on the **Home** tab.

HOW TO DO IT

Word automatically aligns lines of text to the <u>left</u>, but you may want the text to appear on the right or in the middle of the page.

1 Select some text. On the **Home** tab in the "Paragraph" toolset, click the **Center** button. The line moves to the center of the page.

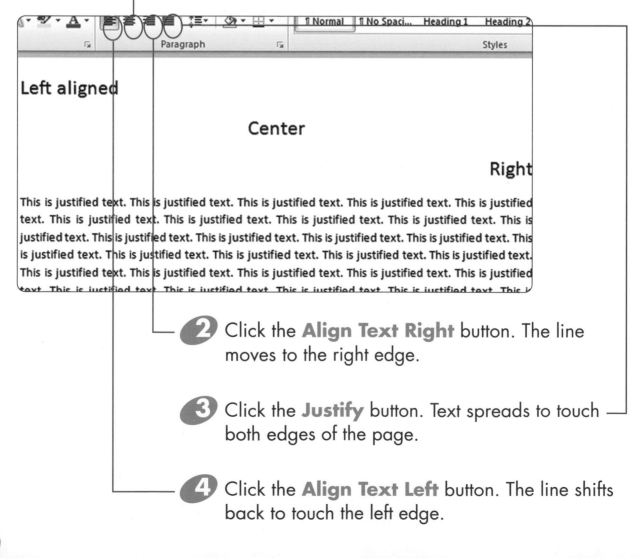

2 Click the **Align Text Right** button. The line moves to the right edge.

3 Click the **Justify** button. Text spreads to touch both edges of the page.

4 Click the **Align Text Left** button. The line shifts back to touch the left edge.

PROJECT 2 GLEE CLUB FLYER

Using alignment on your flyer

Change the alignment of the various parts of your flyer

The flyer is currently aligned to the left. Mix it up a bit.

1 Click on the title and then click on the **Center** button.

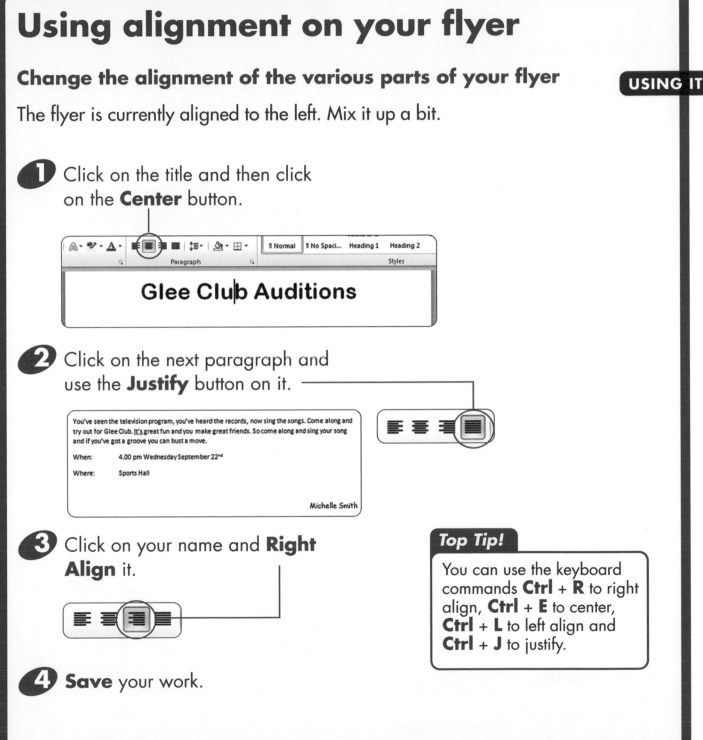

Glee Club Auditions

2 Click on the next paragraph and use the **Justify** button on it.

You've seen the television program, you've heard the records, now sing the songs. Come along and try out for Glee Club. It's great fun and you make great friends. So come along and sing your song and if you've got a groove you can bust a move.

When: 4.00 pm Wednesday September 22ⁿᵈ

Where: Sports Hall

Michelle Smith

3 Click on your name and **Right Align** it.

4 **Save** your work.

> **Top Tip!**
>
> You can use the keyboard commands **Ctrl + R** to right align, **Ctrl + E** to center, **Ctrl + L** to left align and **Ctrl + J** to justify.

White space

Top Tip!

Click the "Paragraph" toolset drop-down menu to explore more options.

Use **Line spacing** and **Indents**

HOW TO DO IT

You can change your document look by increasing space between lines of text or changing where text starts on a line.

1 From the "Paragraph" toolset of the **Home** tab, click the **Line Spacing** button drop-down menu.

2 Select "1.5." The space between lines of text becomes one-and-a-half times bigger.

3 Select "2.0." The space between lines is now <u>double</u> the normal size.

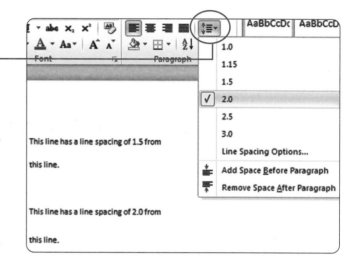

4 Select "Add Space Before Paragraph."

This is a normal paragraph.

This is another normal paragraph.

This paragraph has **Add Space Before Paragraph** added.

≛ Add Space <u>B</u>efore Paragraph

ₜ Remove Space <u>A</u>fter Paragraph

5 The default setting is a space after paragraphs. Select "Remove Space After Paragraph" to remove it.

Remember!

Settings from the "Paragraph" toolset apply to the <u>whole</u> paragraph.

This is a normal paragraph.

This has 1 indent.

This has 2 indents.

6 Click the **Increase Indent** button to start the paragraph farther into the page.

PROJECT 2 GLEE CLUB FLYER

Add some space to the flyer

Adding space between the lines will improve readability

The flyer needs to be really clear.

1 Click on the main block of text and make the line spacing 2.5.

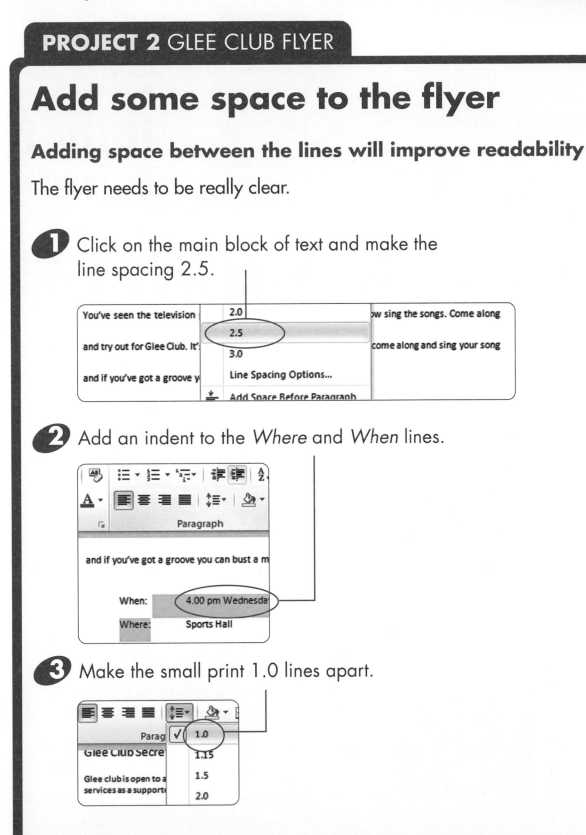

2 Add an indent to the *Where* and *When* lines.

3 Make the small print 1.0 lines apart.

Add some color

Change the **color** of your text

HOW TO DO IT

Word can create really colorful work.

1 Type and select some text in a new document.

2 From the "Font" toolset of the **Home** tab, click the **Font Color** button drop-down menu.

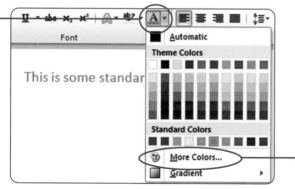

3 Select a green from the "Standard Colors" section.

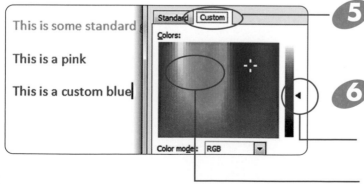

Top Tip!

Colors chosen from the "Colors" dialog box appear in the "Recent" section of the **Font Color** drop-down menu.

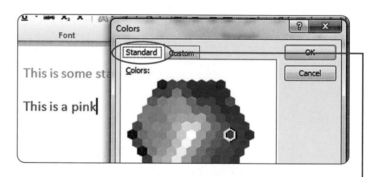

4 Click the **Font Color** button and select "More Colors." This opens the "Colors" dialog box. Choose a pink from the **Standard** tab. Click **OK**. The text has changed color again.

5 Open the "Colors" dialog box again and click the **Custom** tab.

6 Click in the "Colors" area to choose a color. Click-and-drag on the "Brightness Bar" handle to lighten or darken the color. You can see how your color changes.

PROJECT 2 GLEE CLUB FLYER

Brighten the flyer with color

Make the different parts of your poster different colors

USING IT

A bit of color adds interest and excitement to your work.

1 Select the title and make it <u>bright red</u>.

2 Select the main block of text and make it a <u>dark blue</u> from the standard colors.

3 Make *Where* a custom color.

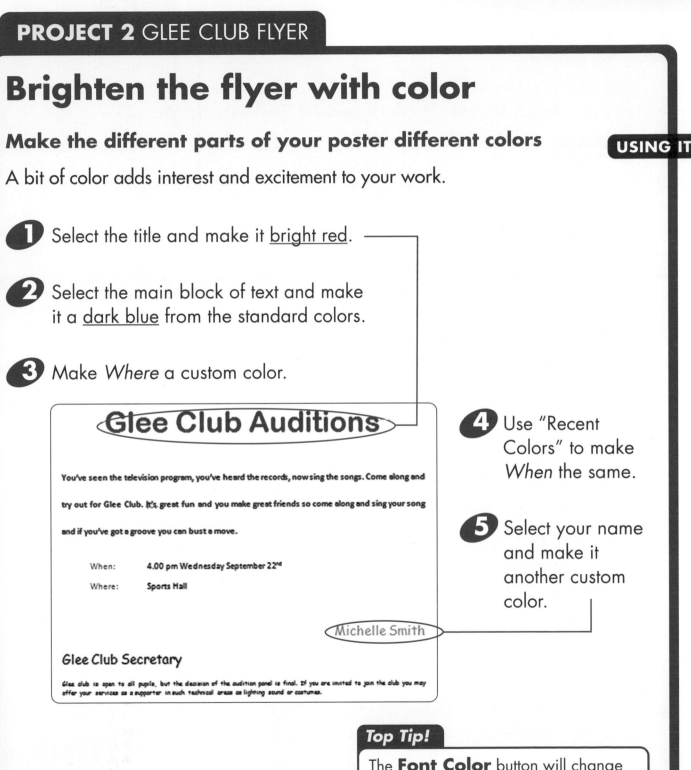

4 Use "Recent Colors" to make *When* the same.

5 Select your name and make it another custom color.

Top Tip!

The **Font Color** button will change the font color to the last one that was set using the drop-down menu.

Be bold

Text styles: Bold, Italics, Underline and Strikethrough

HOW TO DO IT

Text styles are another way of making text interesting and emphasizing particular words or phrases in your document.

1 From the "Font" toolset in the **Home** tab, click the **Bold** button.

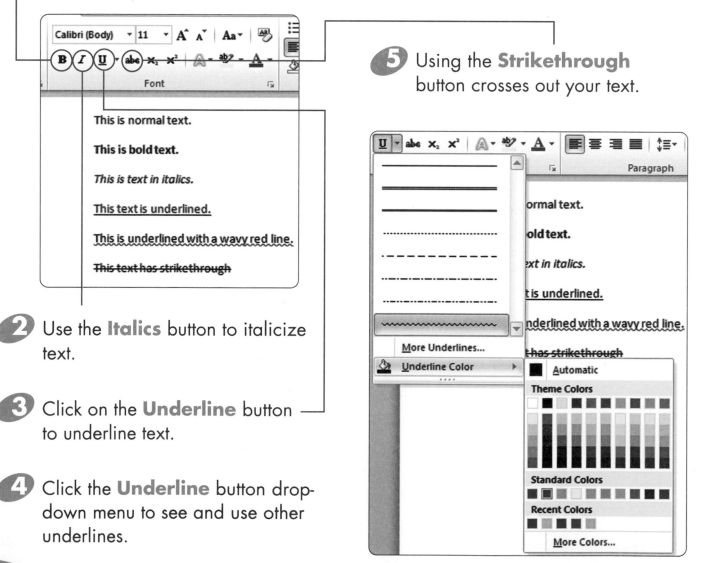

5 Using the **Strikethrough** button crosses out your text.

2 Use the **Italics** button to italicize text.

3 Click on the **Underline** button to underline text.

4 Click the **Underline** button drop-down menu to see and use other underlines.

PROJECT 2 GLEE CLUB FLYER

Apply text styles to the flyer

Use text styles to add emphasis where you need to

The text styles will draw the eye to different parts of the flyer.

USING IT

1 Select the title and make it bold.

2 Use a wavy underline for your name and change the line color to a darker color.

Michelle Smith

3 Italicize the small print at the bottom of the flyer.

Glee Club Secretary

Glee club is open to all pupils, but the decision of th services as a supporter of the club in such technical

4 Use "Strikethrough" to change *great* to *terrific* to *brilliant*.

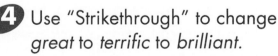

. It's ~~great terrific~~ brilliant fun

Now the highlights

Using the **highlighter**

HOW TO DO IT

Highlighting attracts the reader's attention to important information.

1 The **Highlighter** button either highlights selected text or turns the mouse pointer into the highlighter pen.

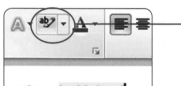

This is highlighted text

2 When the mouse pointer has changed, click-and-drag it over the text you want to highlight.

This is the highlighter in action

3 Click the **Highlighter** button again to turn the highlighter off, or press the **Esc** key.

Remember!

Click-and-drag over text to select it.

4 To use a new color, click the **Highlighter** button drop-down menu and choose a new color.

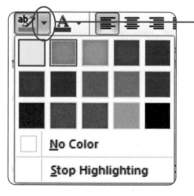

5 To remove highlighting from text, select it and choose **No Color** from the **Highlighter** button drop-down menu.

Highlight parts of your flyer

Make *Where* and *When* stand out

The flyer is starting to look quite busy. Use the "Highlighter" to draw the eye.

1 Select the *Where* and the *When*.

2 Apply the default yellow highlight to them.

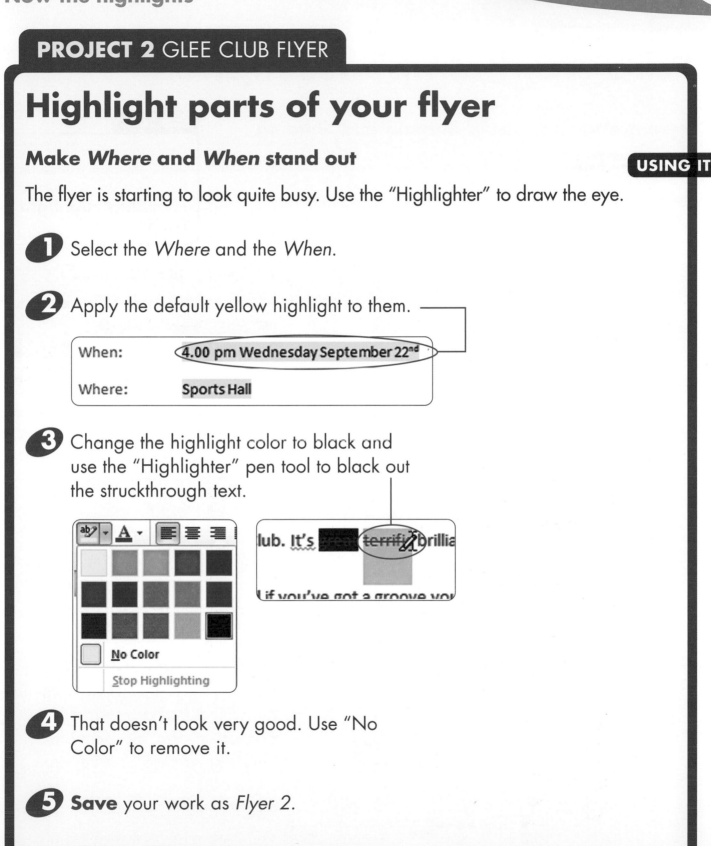

3 Change the highlight color to black and use the "Highlighter" pen tool to black out the struckthrough text.

4 That doesn't look very good. Use "No Color" to remove it.

5 **Save** your work as *Flyer 2*.

Paragraph emphasis options

Style paragraphs using **Borders** and **Shading**

HOW TO DO IT

You can use paragraph shading and borders to color whole paragraphs in one go.

 1 Click into a paragraph on a document.

 2 From the **Home** tab "Paragraph" toolset, click the **Shading** button drop-down menu.

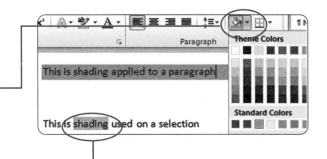

This is shading applied to a paragraph

This is shading used on a selection

 3 Select the color you want. The background of the whole paragraph changes.

4 Select different text and use the **Shading** button to change its background color.

5 To add plain borders, click into a paragraph and then click the **Border** button drop-down menu.

6 To add other borders, click the **Border** button drop-down menu and select **Borders and Shading**. The "Borders and Shading" dialog box appears.

Borders and Shading...

7 You can change the style and color of the border.

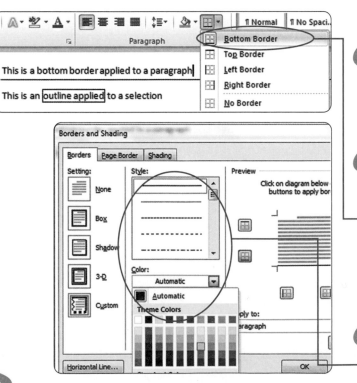

PROJECT 2 GLEE CLUB FLYER

Box and shade your flyer

Apply borders and shading to the flyer

Borders and shading can break up your flyer into different sections.

 Click on the title and give it a bottom border and a background shade of light pink.

> ## Glee Club Auditions

 Select the small print, outline it and shade it light gray.

> Glee club is open to all pupils, but the decision of the audition panel is final. If you are not invited to join the club you may offer your services as a supporter of the club in such technical areas as lighting, sound or costumes.

3 Select the *Where* and *When* lines and use the "Borders and Shading" dialog box to outline them with a 3 point, blue, double line. Use the "Preview" pane to confirm what your shading will look like.

Consistent styles

Using the **Styles** toolset

HOW TO DO IT

Styles are pre-set combinations of "Fonts," "Font sizes," and "Colors." Using styles keeps your **Word** document consistent. If you change the settings for a style, the text in your document changes wherever that style has been used.

1 Select a paragraph.

2 From the **Home** tab, click the **Title** style.

3 That style is now applied to the <u>paragraph</u>.

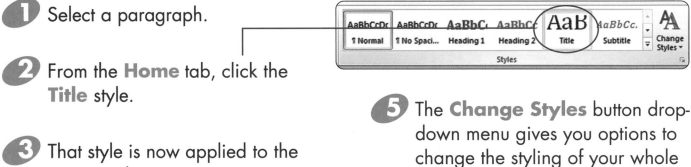

Title style

BOOK TITLE STYLE

Heading 1 style
This is a block of text using the <u>INTENSE REFERENCE</u> style.

4 Select some text and another style from the drop-down menu. That style is applied to the selected <u>text</u>.

MODERN TITLE STYLE

Modern Book Title style

MODERN HEADING 1 STYLE

This is a block of text using the *MODERN INTENSE REFERENCE* style.

5 The **Change Styles** button drop-down menu gives you options to change the styling of your whole document.

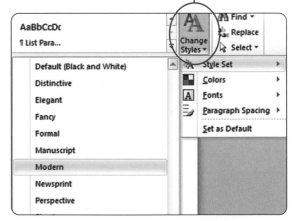

6 Select **Style Set**, **Colors** or **Font** to alter the "Styles" in the current "Set." All existing styles will change and your document will look totally different.

PROJECT 2 GLEE CLUB FLYER

Flyer in styles

Experiment with styles in a copy of the flyer

The flyer already has a number of styles. If we go back to *Flyer 1* we can use the pre-set styles.

 Open *Flyer 1* and click on the title.

 Apply the "Title" style.

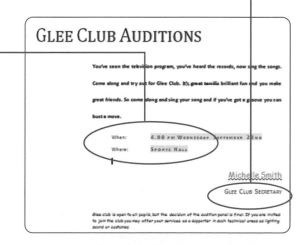

 Select your position and apply the "Subtitle" style.

4 Apply the "Intense Emphasis" style to the *When* and *Where*.

 Use the **Change Styles** button to switch to the "Elegant" style set.

A style of your own

Add your own style to the **Styles** toolset

HOW TO DO IT

The "Styles" built into **Word** give you a wide range of document looks, but they won"t meet all needs.

1 Open a document and select a paragraph of text.

2 Change the "Font" and "Paragraph" settings as shown.

> THIS IS MY NEW STYLE.
>
> GREEN FELIX TITLING 16PT WITH 3 PT BLUE BOTTOM BORDER

3 Click the **Styles** drop-down menu.

4 Select "Save Selection as a New Quick Style".

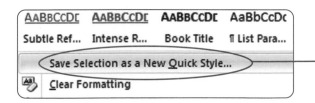

5 Give your new style the name *Green Felix1*. This now appears in the "Styles" toolset.

Create New Style from Formatting

Name:
Green Felix1

Paragraph style preview:

GREEN FELIX1

OK   Modify...   Cancel

AABBC AaBbCcDc AaBbCcDc
Green Feli...   ¶ Normal   ¶ No Spaci...

PROJECT 2 GLEE CLUB FLYER

Use the style given to your name as a Quick Style

Save your style and apply it to your position

Flyer 1 is now looking very stylish, but *Flyer 2* has some appeal as well.

 Open *Flyer 2* and click on your name.

 From the **Styles** drop-down menu, select "Save Selection as a New Quick Style".

Michelle Smith

 Name your new style *MyName*.

Apply your new style to the position text.

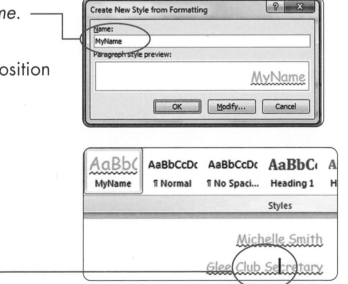

What will it look like?

Print Previewing your work

HOW TO DO IT

"Print Preview" gives you a good idea of what your work will look like when printed.

1 When you are ready to print a document, click on the **File** tab.

2 Click on the **Print** option to view the "Print Area."

3 On the left of the "Print Area" are the **Print** and **Print Settings** options; on the right is the **Print Preview** area.

4 The "Page Turner" at the bottom left of the **Print Preview** area allows you to see what it will look like on each page.

Top Tip!

You can get to the **Print** area by selecting **Print Preview and Print** in the "Quick Access" toolbar. If you don't see the option, click on the drop-down menu and select it.

5 The **Zoom to Page** button at the bottom right of the **Print Preview** area changes the zoom on the preview so you can see the all of the current page.

57%

6 Press **Esc** or click on the **Home** tab to return to your document.

Exit

Prepare the flyer for printing

Check what your flyer will look like when printed

USING IT

Previewing will save printing things unnecessarily.

1 Open *Flyer 2* and go to **Print Screen** in the **File** tab.

2 We need to have the flyer in the middle of the page without too much white space around it. Add lines to the top, increase the font size and make sure the small print is at the bottom of the page.

3 Preview your work as you make the changes to make sure you are improving it.

4 When you are happy with it save it as *Flyer 3*.

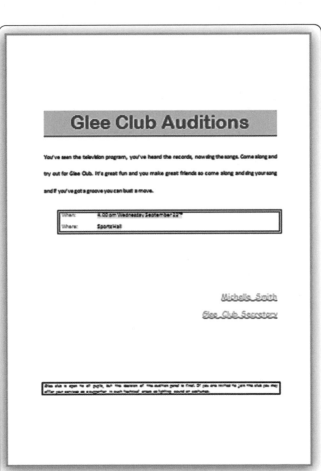

The long or the tall of it

Using different **Orientations**

HOW TO DO IT

A <u>landscape</u> painting is usually wider than it is tall, whereas a <u>portrait</u> is taller than it is wide. You can lay out your documents in the same way.

 Go to the **Print** area on the **File** tab and click on the **Portrait Orientation** button.

 The drop-down menu gives you the two options "Portrait Orientation" (default) and "Landscape Orientation." Select the option you need.

③ The **Print Preview** will be updated automatically.

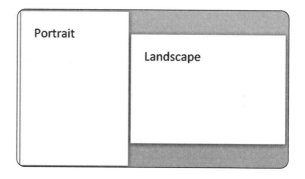

④ Orientation is also available on the **Page Layout** tab.

Challenge!

What do the options under the **1 Page Per Sheet** button do?

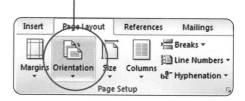

PROJECT 2 GLEE CLUB FLYER

Would the flyer be better in landscape?

Check what orientation is best for the flyer

The flyer has a default portrait orientation, but it could be better in landscape.

1 Open *Flyer 2* and save it as *Flyer 4 Landscape.*

2 Change the orientation to landscape.

3 Make adjustments to it as before, so that it fills the page well.

4 Open *Flyer 3* and decide which is best.

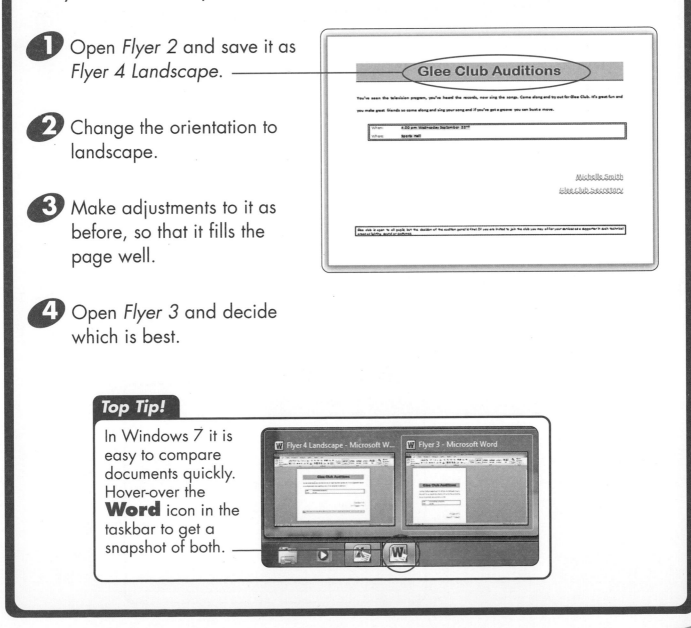

Top Tip!

In Windows 7 it is easy to compare documents quickly. Hover-over the **Word** icon in the taskbar to get a snapshot of both.

Print!

The **Print** button and other printing options

Simple printing is just a click away.

1 At the top of the "Print Area" is the **Print** button.

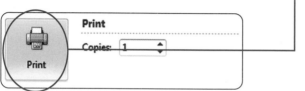

2 You can print off more than one copy by changing the number in the "Copies" field.

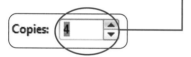

3 You can also use the **Quick Print** button in the "Quick Access Toolbar."

Remember!

To add a button to the "Quick Access Toolbar," select it from the drop-down menu.

PROJECT 2 GLEE CLUB FLYER

Print your flyer

Your first Word document is ready to print

Print both versions of your flyer, then print copies of the one you like best.

1 Open *Flyer 3* and use the **Quick Print** button to print a copy.

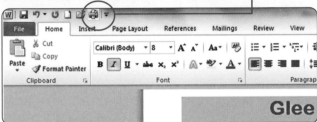

2 Open *Flyer 4 Landscape* and print a copy of that.

3 Choose the version you want to use and increase the number of copies to 5. Print those.

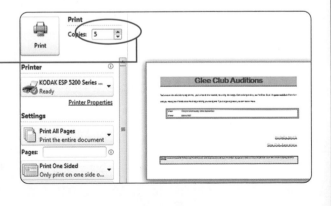

Challenge!

Explore the other **Print Settings** buttons. What will they do for you?

Bullet points

Using **Bullet points**

"Bullet points" make easy-to-read lists.

 Click into a document where you want your list to start.

 In the "Paragraph" toolset of the **Home** tab, click the **Bullet** button.

 A bullet point appears.

4 Type your list. Press the **Enter** key after each item. Notice a bullet point appears at the beginning of each line.

- List Element 1
- List Element 2
- List Element 3
- List Element 4
- |

5 Click the **Bullet** button to stop the bullet points.

6 Click the **Bullet** button drop-down menu to select other styles of bullet point.

Recently Used Bullets

Bullet Library

None

Document Bullets

Change List Level

Define New Bullet...

Top Tip!

You can apply bullet points to lists you have already typed.

Remember!

Use line spacing to space out your list.

PROJECT 3 GET YOUR PARTY PLANNED

What do you need for a great party?

Use bullet points to make a list

Word documents are a great way to make lists.

1 Open a new document.

2 Give your document the heading *My Party* and subtitle *For my party I will need* using different styles.

3 Click the **Bullet** button and list what you need for your party.

4 Click the **Bullet** button and add the second subtitle *These are my guests*.

5 Change the bullet style and list your guests.

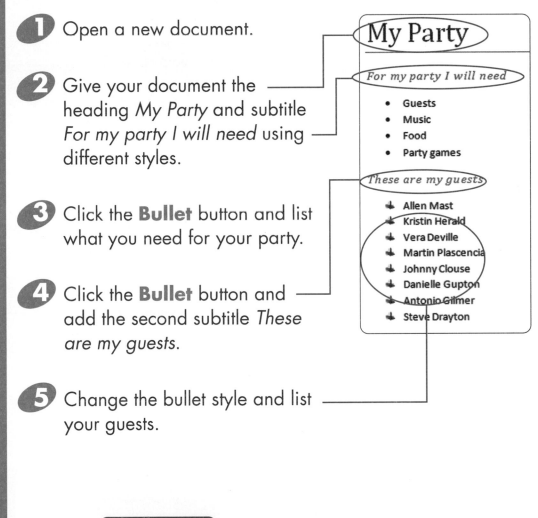

My Party

For my party I will need

- Guests
- Music
- Food
- Party games

These are my guests

↓ Allen Mast
↓ Kristin Herald
↓ Vera Deville
↓ Martin Plascencia
↓ Johnny Clouse
↓ Danielle Gupton
↓ Antonio Gilmer
↓ Steve Drayton

Challenge!

You can create your own bullet styles. Try using "Define New Bullet."

Numbered lists

Using a **Numbered** list

HOW TO DO IT

Bullet points add extra space between lines, but numbered lists keep count of the items as well.

 Start a document.

 In the "Paragraph" toolset on the **Home** tab click the **Numbering** button.

3 1. | will appear.

4 Type your list. Press the **Enter** key after each item.

1. First entry
2. Second entry
3. Third entry
4. Fourth entry

 Click the **Numbering** button to stop numbering.

 Click the **Numbering** button drop-down menu to use other numbering styles.

Recently Used Number Formats

Numbering Library

None

Document Number Formats

Change List Level
Define New Number Format...
Set Numbering Value...

PROJECT 3 GET YOUR PARTY PLANNED

Change the list to use numbers

Bullet points are great, but numbers help keep count

Use numbering when your list needs an order.

 Add the subtitle *What food do I want?* to your party plan.

 Click the **Numbering** button.

3 List the types of food you want.

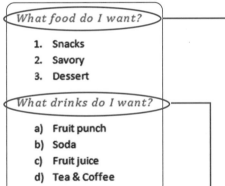

4 Stop numbering and add the new subtitle *What drinks do I want?*

5 Change the numbering style to letters and list the drinks you will need.

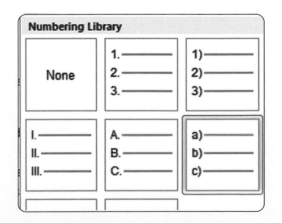

Lists within lists

Create **Multilevel Lists** to add detail

Top Tip!

Select **Clear Formatting** from the "Styles" toolset drop-down menu to remove list formatting.

HOW TO DO IT

It can help to break down your lists into more detail.

 1 Open a new document.

2 In the "Paragraph" toolset of the **Home** tab, click the **Multilevel List** button drop-down menu.

 3 Select a style from the "List Library."

4 Type a list. Press the **Tab** key to move a level <u>in</u> on the list.

 5 Press **Shift** + **Tab** to move <u>out</u> a level.

 6 List styles referring to "Heading" need to be used with "Heading" styles in the "Styles" toolset.

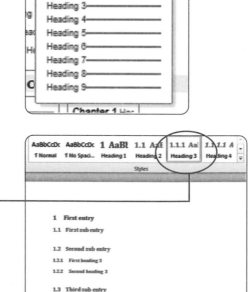

PROJECT 3 GET YOUR PARTY PLANNED

Add detail to your lists

Use multilevel lists to plan your party in greater detail

You have the basic list for your party. Now you need to fill in details.

1 In *My party* planner, click on the first item in your food list.

2 Click the **Multilevel List** button drop-down menu and select a "Numbered List" style. Do not choose a "Heading Style" list.

3 At the end of the first line, press **Enter** then **Tab**.

4 Add a type of snack, e.g. Chips and Dip, click the **Enter** then **Tab** keys to move in to the next level. List the flavors of that snack.

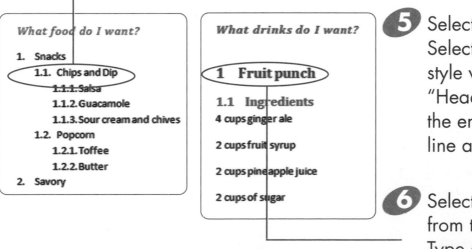

5 Select the drinks list. Select a **Multilevel** style with "Headings." Go to the end of the first line and press **Enter**.

6 Select "Heading 1" from the "Styles" set. Type a subheading then press **Enter**.

Setting the table

Using **Tables** to lay out information

Word has great tools for quick, good-looking tables.

Top Tip!

Pressing the **Tab** key with the cursor in the bottom right cell adds a new row.

 From the **Insert** tab, click the **Table** button drop-down menu.

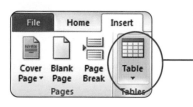

 Select the number of rows and columns you want. This table has 6 columns and 4 rows.

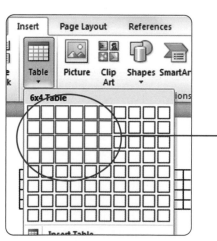

Remember!

Use "Landscape" orientation to print wide tables.

3 The **Table Tools** tab set appears in the ribbon. From the **Design** tab, select a style for your table from the "Table Styles" toolset.

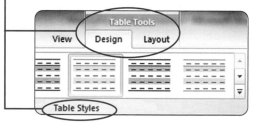

4 Click into the table and start filling it in.

Table with table style				
Column Title				
	Table content			

PROJECT 3 GET YOUR PARTY PLANNED

Create a checklist of party guests

Use tables to make a party checklist

USING IT

Tables can be really useful. Where else would you put the party food? (Joke!)

1 In a new document, *My party checklist*, create a table with one row for each guest, a title row and five columns.

2 Apply a table style.

3 Click in the top left cell and type *Guest*, then add headings to each column.

Guest	Invited	Accepted	Contact Details	Dietary Requirements
Allen Mast				
Kristin Herald				
Vera Deville				
Martin Plascencia				
Johnny Clouse				
Danielle Gupton				
Antonio Gilmer				
Steve Drayton				

My party checklist

4 Add the guests' names in the first column.

Table Tools
Design   Layout

5 Click the "Table Styles' Library" drop-down menu to see all styles.

6 Hover-over table styles to preview the look. Choose a table style.

Table style

Table styles and options

HOW TO DO IT

The **Table Tools – Design** tab gives you options for changing your table.

1 The "Table Style Options" toolset of the **Design** tab allows you to change the formatting of table styles.

2 Setting the "First Column" and "Last Column" and "Header Row" options adds emphasis.

3 The "Banded" column and row options add color to alternate rows and columns.

4 You can change the color and borders of cells by choosing from the **Shading** button drop-down menu.

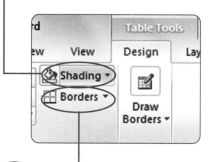

5 You can add border styles to cells by choosing from the **Borders** button drop-down menu.

PROJECT 3 GET YOUR PARTY PLANNED

Create a checklist for your party guests

Style your party checklist for easy reading

You can make your table clearer so that information is easy to find.

1 Click into your checklist to bring up the **Table Design** tab on the ribbon.

2 Make sure the "Header Row," "First Column" and "Banded Rows" are the only options selected.

3 Select the "Dietary Requirements" column. Change the background color to dark blue.

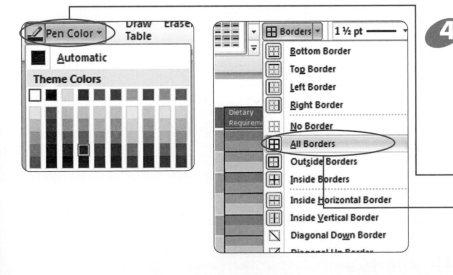

4 Give the column large borders. Click the **Border Line Weight** button drop-down menu to set to 3 point. Change the **Pen Color** to dark blue and select "All Borders" from the **Border** button drop-down menu.

Table changes

Top Tip!

You can click-and-drag the columns in the ruler at the top of the screen to quickly change column width.

Inserting/Deleting/AutoFitting rows and columns

HOW TO DO IT

Tools for designing tables are on the **Layout** tab.

1 To add a row or column, click in the table where you want to add it.

2 In the "Rows & Columns" toolset of the **Layout** tab, click the appropriate **Insert** button.

3 To delete a row or column, click on it; then in the "Rows & Columns" toolset click on the **Delete** button.

4 Select the delete option you need, e.g. **Delete Columns**.

5 To change a row or column size, select a cell within it. Then in the "Cell Size" toolset of the **Layout** tab, increase the height of the row or width of the column.

6 The **AutoFit Contents** option changes the column sizes to fit the text in each column. **AutoFit Window** adjusts the table to fit the page width.

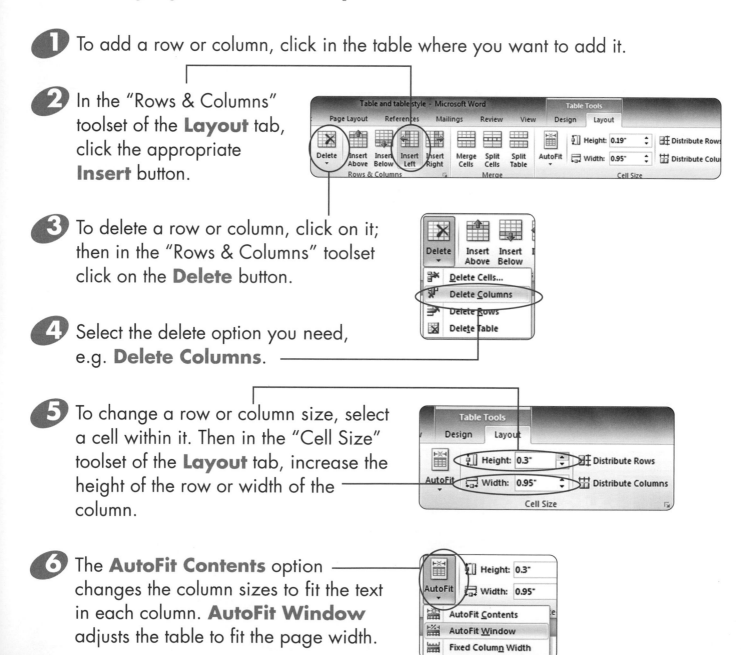

PROJECT 3 GET YOUR PARTY PLANNED

Change your party checklist

Adjusting the columns

USING IT

Alter your checklist to meet your changing needs.

1 Add a column to the end of your table to record the presents your guests bring.

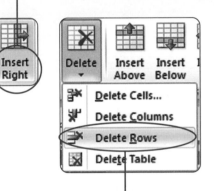

2 Delete one of your guests who cannot come.

3 Make the last column wider.

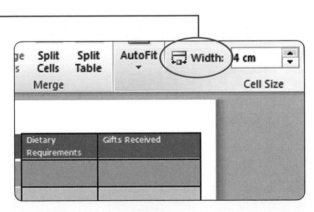

4 Change the document orientation to "Landscape" and then use **AutoFit Window** to space out the other columns.

Other table tools

Merging/Splitting Cells and Text Direction

HOW TO DO IT

Top Tip!
Using the eraser in the **Draw Table** section is the same as merging cells.

You can do many other things with tables. These options help you put the information in the right places.

 To merge cells into one, select the cells then click the **Merge Cells** button in the "Merge" toolset of the **Layout** tab.

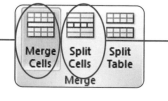

 To split cells after they have been merged, or to add cells within a cell, use the **Split Cells** button.

 This gives you the option to choose how many columns and rows you want to split the cell into.

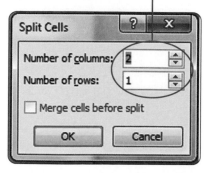

4 You may want to change your text direction, for example, if you need text at the top of narrow columns. In the **Layout** tab "Alignment" toolset, click the **Text Direction** button.

5 Click once to write from top to bottom. Click again to write from bottom to top. Use the **Alignment** buttons to align text within a cell.

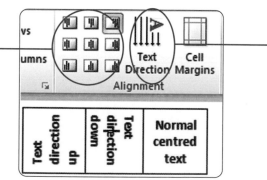

Remember!
Save your work as you go along. You don't want to lose anything!

Final touches for your checklist

Add merged title rows to your columns

Using layout tab options in your checklist.

 Add a column to the left of the checklist.

 Make the column narrower then merge the cells together.

 Make the text direction bottom to top and type *Guests*. Center this in the cell.

Guests		Invited	Accepted	Contact Details	Dietary Requirements	Gifts Received
	Allen Mast					
	Kristin Herald					
	Vera Deville					
	Martin Plascencia					
	Johnny Clouse					
	Danielle Gupton					
	Antonio Gilmer					
	Steve Drayton					

My party checklist

4 Make the text direction of *Invited* and *Accepted* top to bottom.

5 Make the *Invited* and *Accepted* columns very narrow.

USING IT

Copy and paste

Repeat something without having to retype it

HOW TO DO IT

Duplicating text is quicker than typing it again.

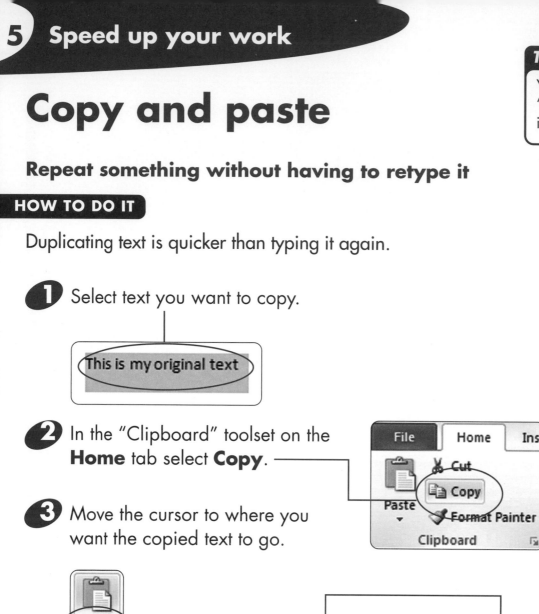

1 Select text you want to copy.

This is my original text

2 In the "Clipboard" toolset on the **Home** tab select **Copy**.

3 Move the cursor to where you want the copied text to go.

Paste

4 Click the **Paste** button.

This is my original text

Now I can type some more

Then paste – This is my original text

5 The copied text appears there.

PROJECT 4 PARTY THANKS

Copy and paste from your checklist

Use copy and paste to save time

Doing boring jobs can be made quicker using copy and paste.

1 Open your *My Party* planning document.

2 Open a new document. Save it as *Party Thanks*.

Madeleine E Zee

835 Meadow Drive

Moore, OK 73160

Dear

3 Start typing a thank you letter.

4 When you need a name from the party plan, switch to the *My Party* document and select the name (turn off the bullet points first).

These are my guests

Allen Mast

Kristin Herald

Vera Deville

5 Copy the name, then switch back to your letter.

6 Click where you want the name to go and paste it into place.

Dear Allen

Moving

Move your work around

HOW TO DO IT

"Cut" and "Paste" help you to reorganize work.

1 Select the text you want to move.

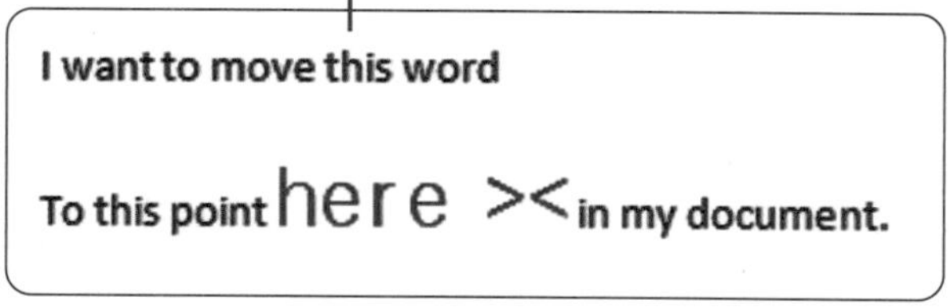

I want to move this word

To this point here >< in my document.

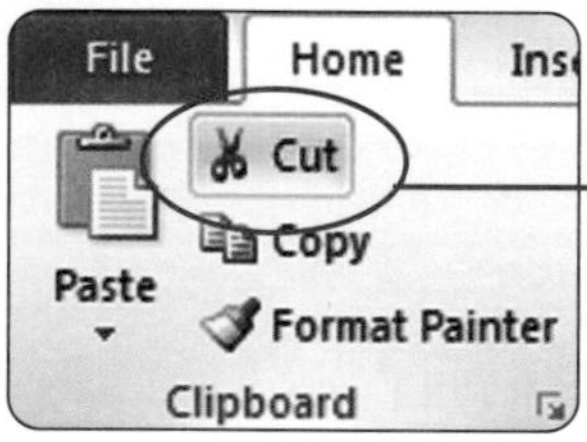

2 Click **Cut** from the "Clipboard" toolset. The text disappears.

> File   Home   Ins
> ✂ Cut
> 📋 Copy
> Paste   🖌 Format Painter
> Clipboard

3 Click where you want the text to go.

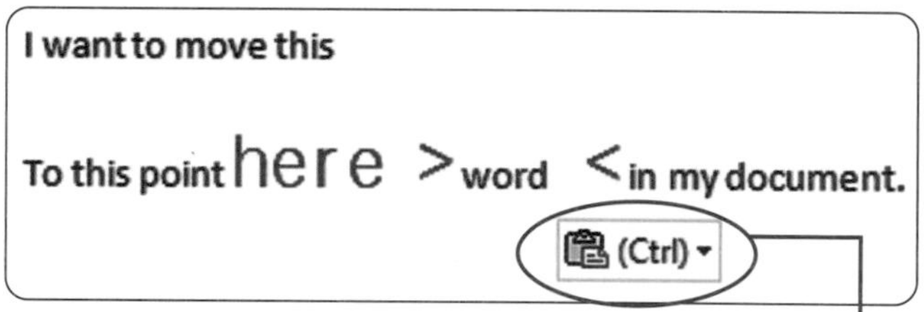

I want to move this

To this point here >word < in my document.

📋 (Ctrl) ▾

4 Select **Paste**. The text reappears in the new position.

5 If the text is a different <u>style</u> at the new position, use the **Paste options** drop-down menu that appears next to the pasted text and select **Merge Formatting**.

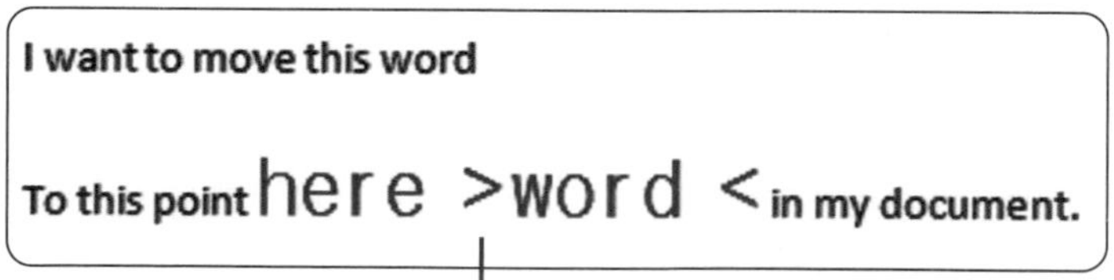

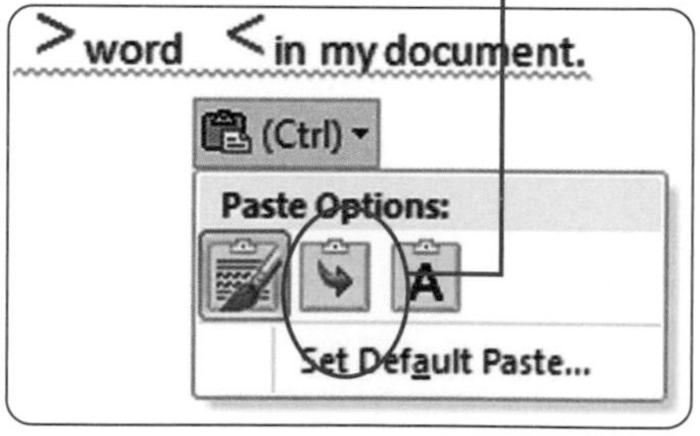

I want to move this word

To this point here >word < in my document.

> word < in my document.

📋 (Ctrl) ▾
Paste Options:

Set Default Paste...

6 The pasted text is now the same style as the surrounding text.

PROJECT 4 PARTY THANKS

Move your letter text around

Use cut and paste to rearrange your thank you letter

Moving text around allows you to see how well different orders of text read.

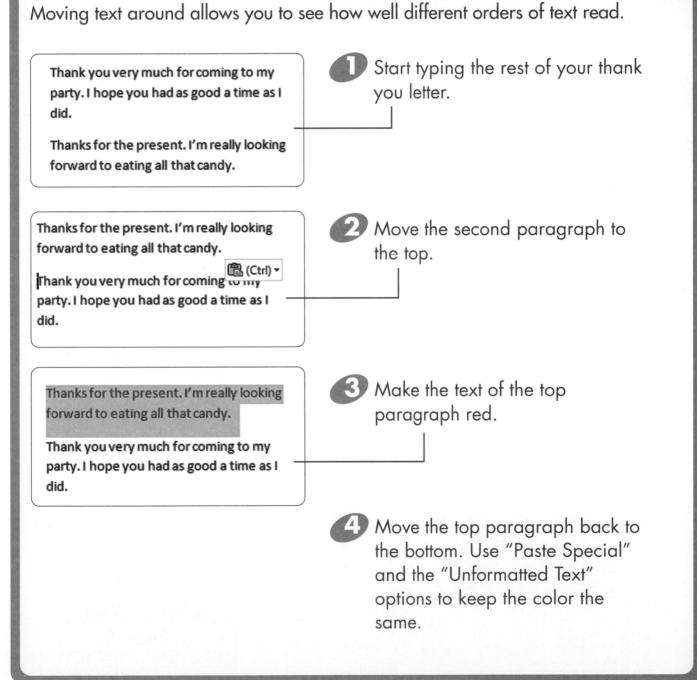

Thank you very much for coming to my party. I hope you had as good a time as I did.

Thanks for the present. I'm really looking forward to eating all that candy.

1 Start typing the rest of your thank you letter.

Thanks for the present. I'm really looking forward to eating all that candy.

(Ctrl) ▾

Thank you very much for coming to my party. I hope you had as good a time as I did.

2 Move the second paragraph to the top.

Thanks for the present. I'm really looking forward to eating all that candy.

Thank you very much for coming to my party. I hope you had as good a time as I did.

3 Make the text of the top paragraph red.

4 Move the top paragraph back to the bottom. Use "Paste Special" and the "Unformatted Text" options to keep the color the same.

Turn back time

Using the Undo, Redo and Repeat buttons

HOW TO DO IT

It's easy to make a mistake, and just as easy to correct it –
even if correcting the mistake was a mistake!

 Type your name into a document.

 From the "Quick Access" toolbar,
click the **Undo** button.

3 Your name disappears. To undo
more than one mistake, keep clicking
the **Undo** button.

4 Or click the **Undo** button drop-down
menu.

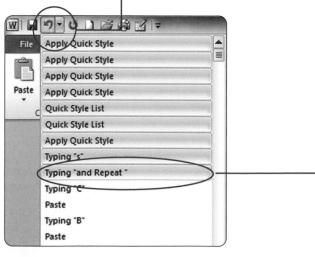

5 A list of your recent actions
appears. Click the last action
you want to undo.

6 If you decide you don't want to
undo something after all, click
the **Redo** button. You can keep
clicking this until you are back
to the start.

7 If you haven't undone anything,
the **Redo** button becomes the
Repeat button; it repeats
your last action.

PROJECT 4 PARTY THANKS

Put it back as it was

Moving stuff around can cause problems

Let's undo the paragraph swaps on the thank you letter.

USING IT

1 Click the **Undo** button to swap the paragraphs back.

2 Click the **Undo** button drop-down menu to see all the actions done so far.

3 Undo back to the original plain text letter. Undo to the first "Clear."

4 Click the **Redo** button to get the first color change back.

Dear Allen,

Thanks for the present. I'm really looking forward to eating all that candy.

Thank you very much for coming to my party. I hope you had as good a time as I did.

Best Regards

Madeleine

The history of copying

Using the Clipboard

HOW TO DO IT

The "Clipboard" allows you to reuse anything that you have copied in Microsoft Office and other compatible programs, not just **Word**.

1 Open the *My Party* list document and copy some of the food list.

2 From the "Clipboard" toolset on the **Home** tab, select the toolset drop-down menu.

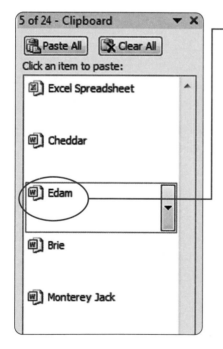

3 Find the "clip" that you want to paste.

4 Click on it to paste it into your document.

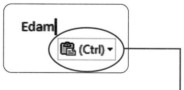

5 Click on the "Paste Options" pop-up panel and select "Match Destination Formatting" to apply the surrounding formatting.

Remember!

If you have moved something, it has been copied first.

PROJECT 4 PARTY THANKS

Paste from the Clipboard

Use the Clipboard to create lots of thank you letters

Once the names are on the Clipboard, it's easy to churn out thank you letters.

USING IT

1 Open your party planning document.

2 Select the name of each guest and copy it.

Top Tip!

Double-click on a word to select it without clicking-and-dragging over it.

3 Open the Clipboard.

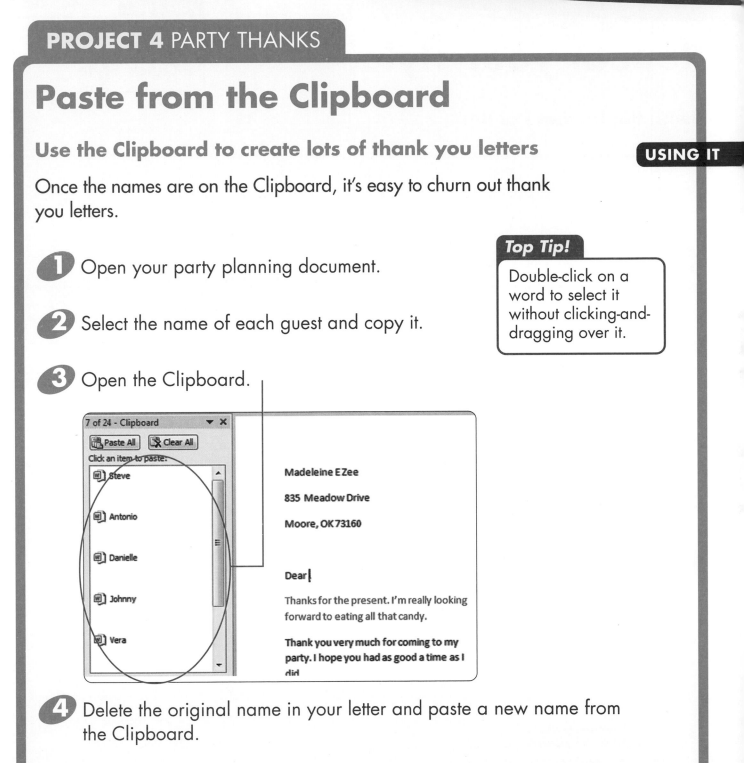

4 Delete the original name in your letter and paste a new name from the Clipboard.

5 Save the thank you letter with a new file name. Reopen the original thank you letter and repeat so that you have a letter for each guest.

Repeat your style

Top Tip!

If you are going to use the style a lot, make it a **Quick Style**.

Using the **Format Painter**

HOW TO DO IT

We have copied and pasted text. The "Format Painter" copies styles.

 1 In a document, click on text with the format you want to copy.

This is a nice style
....
I want this text to look the same

2 Click the **Format Painter** button. The selected formatting is copied and the mouse pointer changes to a paintbrush.

I want the text to look the same

3 Move the "Format Painter" over the text you want to copy the format to.

4 Click-and-drag over the text you want to change.

5 The "Format Painter" works once only. Click the button again if you want to repeat using it. Press **Esc** if you don't want to use it after all.

Remember!

The "Repeat" button will repeat a style change if that was your last action.

I want this text to look the same

PROJECT 4 PARTY THANKS

Spread your style about

Your letters look a bit dull

Use the "Format Painter" to change the format of your thank you letters.

1 Select the letter text.

2 Change the font, font size and font color to *Bradley Hand ITC*, 14 point, dark blue text.

> Madeleine & Zee
>
> 835 Meadow Drive
>
> Moore, OK 73160
>
>
> Dear Allen,
>
> Thanks for the present. I'm really looking forward to eating all that candy.
>
> Thank you very much for coming to my party. I hope you had as good a time as I did.
>
> Best Regards

3 Open another letter.

4 Switch back to the first letter.

5 Click in the letter, then click the **Format Painter** button.

6 Switch back to the second letter and paste the format over it all.

> Madeleine & Zee
>
> 835 Meadow Drive
>
> Moore, OK 73160
>
>
> Dear Danielle,
>
> Thanks for the present. I'm really looking to reading the book you gave me.

What's the time?

Inserting the time or date and other symbols

HOW TO DO IT

Word makes life easier with some quick tools.

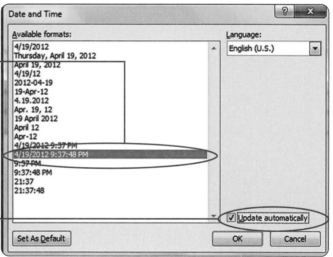

1 Click where you want the date or time to go.

2 From the "Text" toolset on the **Insert** tab, click the **Date & Time** button. The "Date & Time" dialog box appears.

3 Select the format you need.

4 If you want the date or time to be the current one, tick "Update automatically."

5 The date and time will update when you reopen the document, or you can click on it and then select the **Update** tab that appears.

6 Click the **Symbol** button drop-down menu on the **Insert** tab.

7 Select one of the symbols, e.g. the © symbol from the "Symbol" dialog box that appears. This will insert it into your text.

PROJECT 4 PARTY THANKS

Add the date to your letter

Add a date and some symbols to your letters

Use the insert options to improve your letters.

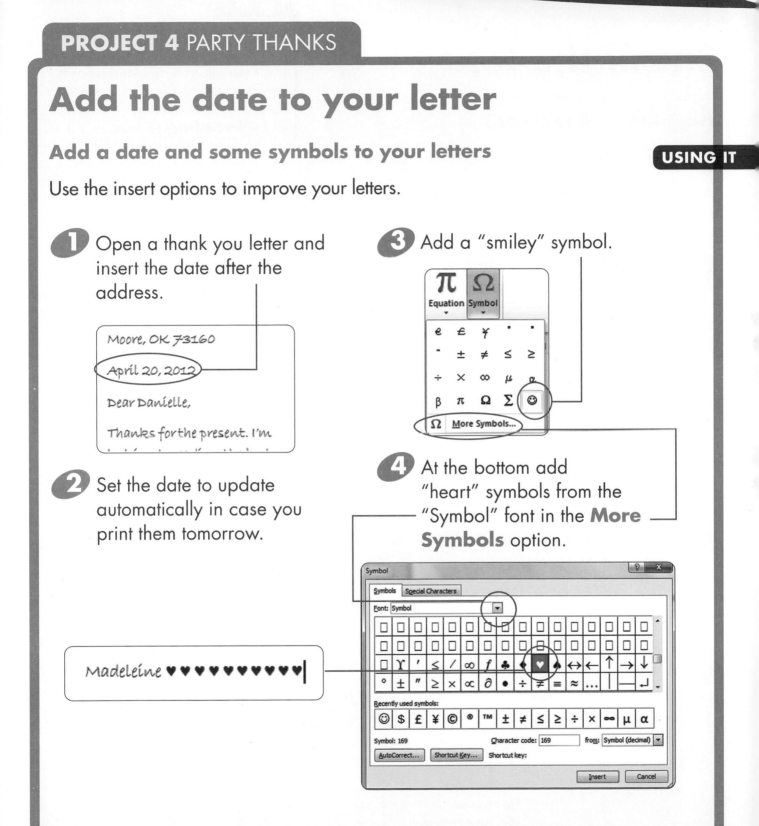

1 Open a thank you letter and insert the date after the address.

Moore, OK 73160

April 20, 2012

Dear Danielle,

Thanks for the present. I'm

2 Set the date to update automatically in case you print them tomorrow.

Madeleine ♥♥♥♥♥♥♥♥♥♥|

3 Add a "smiley" symbol.

4 At the bottom add "heart" symbols from the "Symbol" font in the **More Symbols** option.

Check the text

Using the spell checker

"Grammar tips" can be hard to get rid of. Use **Word options** from the **File** tab to hide them. Click to remove the tick from the "Check grammar with spelling" check box in the **Proofing** section.

Squiggly red or green lines appear under some words to show that **Word** thinks they may be a spelling or grammar mistake.

 1 If a squiggly line appears under a word, right-click on it.

 2 If it is a <u>red</u> line, this menu will appear.

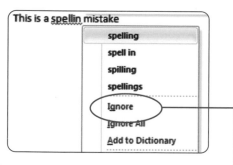

3 Choose the correct spelling from the options. If the spelling you have used is OK, select **Ignore**. Select "Add to Dictionary" if you often use this word.

4 If it's a <u>green</u> line then it's a grammar mistake. **Word** will offer you an alternative or will tell you what it thinks is wrong.

5 To check a <u>whole</u> document, click the **Spelling & Grammar** button in the **Review** tab. **Word** brings up the "Spelling and Grammar" dialog box and shows each query.

PROJECT 4 PARTY THANKS

Check your spelling

It's quick and easy to get it right

There is no excuse for bnad spulling with a "Spell Checker"!

1 Right-click on and correct anything with a red spelling alert.

> Dear Johnny,
>
> Thanks for the present. Its really nice. I'm really looking forward to playin with my new toy.
>
> Thank you very much for coming to my party. I hope you

playing
plain
play in
Ignore
Ignore All
Add to Dictionary
AutoCorrect ▶
Language ▶
Spelling...
Look Up | ▶
Cut
Copy
Paste Options:
Additional Actions ▶

2 Right-click on and correct anything with a green grammar alert.

> Dear Johnny,
>
> Thanks for th
> nice. I'm reall
> to playin wit

Dear Johnny
Ignore Once
Grammar...
About This Sentence

3 Double check everything. Bring up the "Spelling and Grammar" dialog box and check the whole document.

for the present. Its really

Spelling and Grammar: English (U.S.)

Possible Word Choice Error:

Its really nice.

Ignore Once
Ignore All
Add to Dictionary

Suggestions:

It's

Change
Change All

Another word for thesaurus

Using the **Thesaurus**

HOW TO DO IT

Word has a great tool for alternatives to words, e.g. *wonderful* and *fantastic* are alternatives to *terrific*.

 Click on the word you want an alternative for, e.g. *great*.

 In the **Review** tab, click the **Thesaurus** button in the "Proofing" toolset.

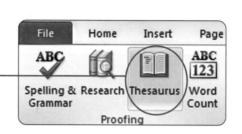

3 The "Research" dialog box opens.

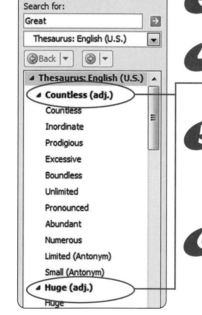

4 The **Thesaurus** shows alternatives to the word. The different headings depend on the word's meaning.

5 Hover-over the word you want to use; a drop-down menu appears. Click the drop-down arrow.

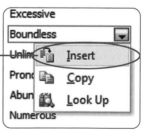

6 Select **Insert** to add that word to your document or **Copy** to use it later. **Look Up** will find more alternatives.

Remember!

Save the original word to the "clipboard" if you are not sure you want to change the word.

PROJECT 4 PARTY THANKS

Make your language more interesting

It's a bad habit always to use the same word

Make your thank you letter more interesting and expand your vocabulary with the Thesaurus.

1 Open a thank you letter.

> Thank you very much for coming to my party. I hope you had as good a time as I did.
>
> Best Regards

2 Click on a common word like *good*.

3 Check the list of alternatives.

4 Hover-over the one you want to use and insert it in your letter.

> coming to my party. I hope you had as lovely a time as I did.

Find out more

Word links to the internet to help **Research** your work

HOW TO DO IT

The **Research** button finds information on the internet.

1 Select the word(s) you want more information about.

Endangered animals

2 Click the **Research** button on the **Review** tab.

Top Tip!

Clicking while pressing the **Alt** key automatically opens the **Research** window.

3 You will get a list of web sites. Click the drop-down arrow and select the one you want to check.

4 Click on a link to see that web page.

Remember!

You can also use *Yahoo!* or *Google* and copy information into your document.

PROJECT 4 PARTY THANKS

Want to know more?

The internet has lots of information for you

The **Research** button makes it easy to show that you really liked your presents!

1 Click on the word you want to study.

being a sponsor
dolphin!

2 Look up the word on a research site.

3 Find some interesting information from the links.

4 Use your new knowledge to improve your letter.

dolphin! Out of the nearly forty
species of dolphin, Amazon river
dolphins are the most
endangered.

Research ▾ ✕

Search for:

dolphin →

Bing ▾

⊕ Back ▾   ⊕ ▾

▲ **Bing (1-10 of 27300000)** ▲

Next

bing

▸ **Dolphin - Wikipedia, the free encyclopedia**
Dolphins are marine mammals that are closely related to whales and porpoises. There are almost forty species of dolphin in seventeen genera. They vary in size from 1 ...
en.wikipedia.org/wiki/Dolphi

▸ **dolphin: Definition from Answers.com**
dolphin n. , pl. , dolphin , or -phins . Any of various marine cetacean mammals,

Adding graphics

Add photographs and other pictures

With digital cameras and the internet, it's easy to put pictures into a document.

 Click where you want a picture to go.

 From the **Insert** tab, click the **Picture** button. The "Insert Picture" dialog box appears.

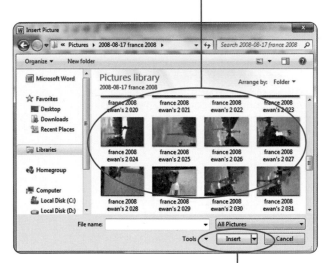

3 Find a picture on your computer, then click **Insert**. The picture appears in your document.

Top Tip!
You can copy and paste pictures to move them around.

4 Click-and-drag the <u>corners</u> to change the size of your picture. Click-and-drag the <u>green dot</u> to rotate it.

Remember!
Use the **View** button on the "Insert Picture" dialog box to see available pictures.

PROJECT 5 SCHOOL FAIR POSTER

Add a picture of your school

Use pictures to smarten up a poster

Pictures are an excellent way to make your poster eye-catching.

 Open a new document.

 Insert a picture into your poster.

3 Make the picture smaller.

4 Rotate the picture to make it look wacky!

Playing with pictures

Changing pictures after you have added them

The **Picture Tools – Format** tab has lots of options for styling your picture. Add borders, picture effects or captions.

 1 To add a border, click on the picture and select a border from the "Picture Styles" toolset.

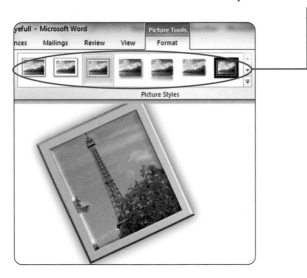

 2 Change picture frame color using the **Picture Border** button.

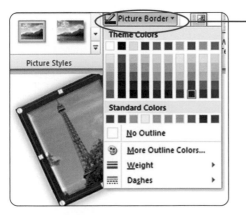

 3 The **Picture Layout** button allows you to organize your pictures with captions.

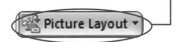 **4** The **Picture Effects** button adds cool effects.

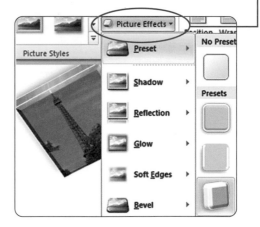

Remember!
Undo is your friend.

PROJECT 5 SCHOOL FAIR POSTER

Make the picture stand out

A good frame defines a picture

Make the picture stand out against the white background.

1 Click on your picture.

2 Give it a bevelled oval style.

3 Give the frame a colorful border.

4 Select a **Reflection** picture effect.

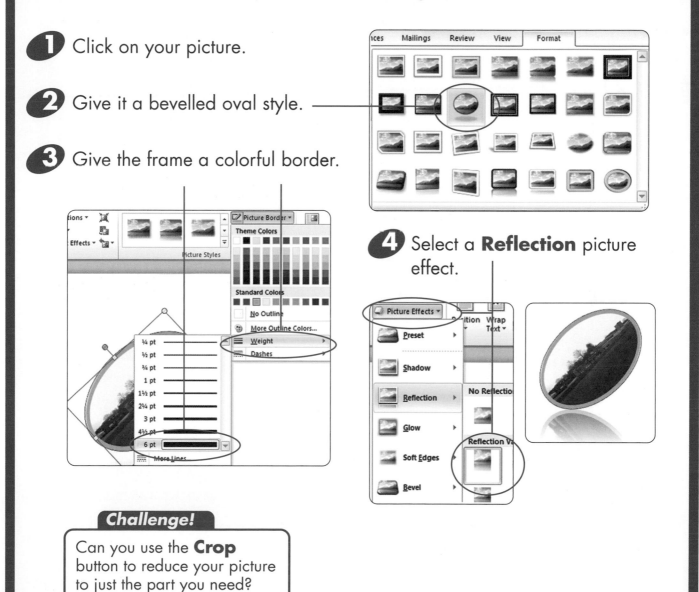

Challenge!

Can you use the **Crop** button to reduce your picture to just the part you need?

Clipping an image from another screen

HOW TO DO IT

Use the **Screenshot button**

Word has a tool for capturing images from your computer screen.

 From the **Insert** tab, **Illustrations** toolset, click on the **Screenshot** tool.

 The drop-down menu shows all the windows you have open.

3 Select the window you want and an image of it will be inserted in your worksheet.

4 Select the **Screen Clipping** tool from the drop-down menu if you only want to capture part of the screen.

5 The **Word** window will minimize and the screen will turn opaque. Click-and-drag the mouse over the area you want to capture and that image will be inserted into your worksheet.

PROJECT 5 SCHOOL FAIR POSTER

Add a picture from your school web site

Use **Screenshot** to capture something from the web

The internet is full of great images. Screenshot brings them straight into your document.

1 Click into your poster document and press **Enter** to add new lines.

2 Open your internet browser and go to your school web site.

3 Find the image you want to capture and switch back to **Word**. Click on the **Screen Clipping** button.

4 Add a "Picture Style" and a "Soft Edge" Picture Effect.

Clip Art

Word comes with cartoons

Top Tip!

If you use a button like **Clip Art** a lot, right click on it and then click on **Add to Quick Access Toolbar**.

"Clip Art" is pictures built into **Word** for you to use. If you need more images, there is also a library of Clip Art on the internet.

 Click into the document where you want the Clip Art to go.

 From the **Insert** tab "Illustrations" toolset, click the **Clip Art** button.

 The "Clip Art" dialog box opens.

4 Type what sort of picture you want in the **Search for** field, then click **Go**.

5 You will get more choices if you are connected to the internet and the **Include Office.com content** option is ticked.

6 Limit your search to just pictures by selecting "Illustrations" only in the **media file types** field.

7 To use a Clip Art picture, click on it.

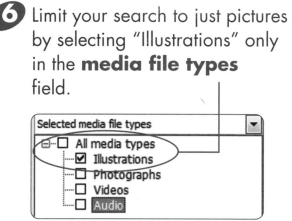

PROJECT 5 SCHOOL FAIR POSTER

Insert some Clip Art

Cartoons are always fun

Clip Art is available for almost any subject.
Use it to brighten up your poster.

 Search for Clip Art related to
your school fair.

 Click on the poster where you
want the Clip Art to go.

 Insert the picture.

 Resize, rotate and add borders
to match the other picture.

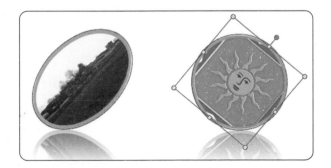

Inserting shapes

Arrows, other **shapes** and speech bubbles

HOW TO DO IT

As well as Clip Art, **Word** has <u>shapes</u> you can use.

1 Click the **Shapes** button.

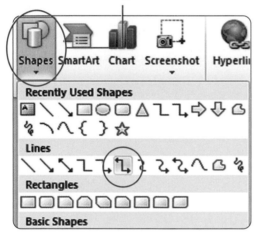

2 Select the shape you want to use.

3 Click-and-drag the shape to where you want it.

Use Arrows to link one bit of text

to another

4 The **Drawing Tools – Format** tab opens on the ribbon, allowing you to change the shapes, colors, widths and styles of the shapes.

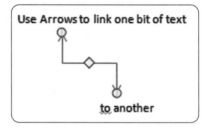

PROJECT 5 SCHOOL FAIR POSTER

Add a speech bubble to the picture

Use shapes to customize your pictures

Shapes allow you to draw on your poster.

 Add a square speech bubble "Callouts" shape to your poster.

 Click-and-drag it so the speech bubble is coming out of the picture.

 Click into the speech bubble and start typing.

4 Insert an arrow between your picture and the Clip Art.

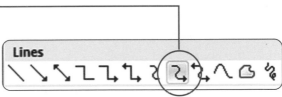

5 Use a "Shape Style" from the **Format** tab to increase the size of the arrow.

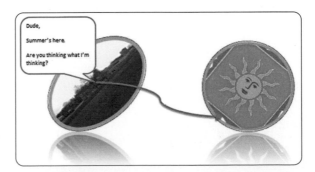

Text boxes

Add a block of text that you can move around

HOW TO DO IT

"Text Boxes" are a smart way of adding blocks of text.

Top Tip!

Text boxes can go anywhere that the "Insert" point can go. If you have a new document, press the **Enter** key until you get to the bottom of the page.

 From the **Insert** tab, click the **Text Box** button drop-down menu.

 Select a text box style. This one's called *Austere Sidebar.*

3 Click into the text box and type your text.

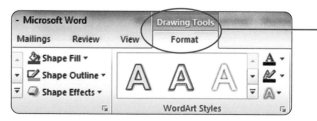

4 The **Drawing Tools – Format** tab opens so you can change the format of the text box.

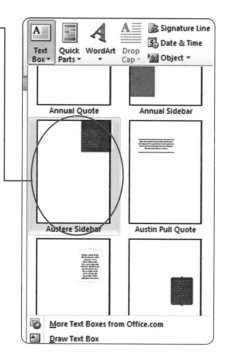

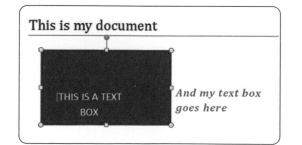

5 Click-and-drag the text box to move it, or click on the corners to change the size.

Remember!

Click the **Home** tab to change the font and paragraph style of your text.

PROJECT 5 SCHOOL FAIR POSTER

Add a text box to your poster

Add a text box with details of the fair

A text box helps to distinguish text from the rest of the document.

 Click at the bottom of your poster.

 Insert a text box. Use the *Mod Quote* style.

 Use the **Format** button to change the style to match the rest of your poster. Add a *Soft Glow* effect to jazz it up.

 The **Font** toolset in the **Home** tab can be used on the text in the box. Make the text bigger and bold.

③ Insert the date and time of the fair into the text box.

Outstanding text effects

Use **WordArt** in a document

HOW TO DO IT

"WordArt" gives colorful effects to your text.

1 Open a new document.

2 From the **Insert** tab, click the **WordArt** button drop-down menu.

3 Select a WordArt style.

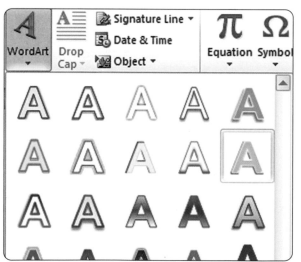

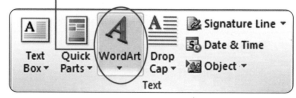

Remember!

Hover-over a style option to preview it.

4 A WordArt text area appears at the insert point in your document. Type your WordArt text.

5 The **WordArt Tools – Format** tab opens, giving you formatting options.

Go wild with the title

Use WordArt to give your poster a big title

WordArt can make your text look amazing.

1 Click in your poster where you want your title.

2 Select a style and type your title in the dialog box.

3 Modify the style using the options in the "WordArt Style" toolset.

4 This one has "Bevel," "Reflection," and "Transform" text effects.

Working around your graphics

Wrapping text around an object

HOW TO DO IT

Pictures and WordArt use a single line in your document. "Wrapping" lets you make them part of the text.

1 Click on the object you want to wrap text around.

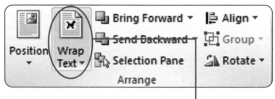

2 From the **Format** tab, click the **Wrap Text** button drop-down menu.

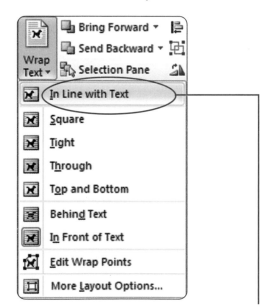

3 Select a "Wrap" option. The default is **In Line with Text**. The icons show you how the text wrap will look.

4 These are some "Wrap" options.

Square

Tight

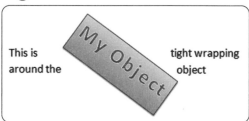

In Front of Text

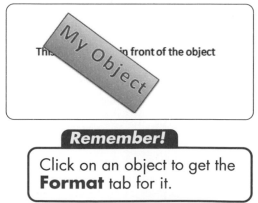

PROJECT 5 SCHOOL FAIR POSTER

Wrap some more text around the text box

Use wrap text to run text around the fair details text box on the poster

Without wrapping, inserted objects such as WordArt and text boxes get in the way of the main document.

1 Click on the text box.

2 Set wrap to **Tight**.

3 Click on the poster to the left of the text box.

4 Type out the attractions at your fair.

USING IT

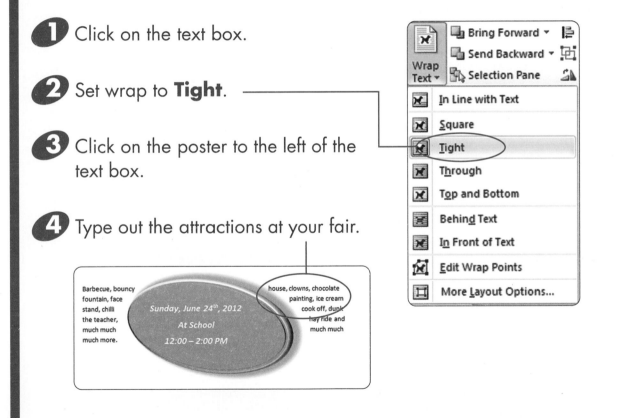

Wrap Text ▾

🔲 Bring Forward ▾
🔲 Send Backward ▾
🔲 Selection Pane

▣ In Line with Text
▣ Square
▣ Tight
▣ Through
▣ Top and Bottom
▣ Behind Text
▣ In Front of Text
▣ Edit Wrap Points
▣ More Layout Options...

Barbecue, bouncy fountain, face stand, chilli the teacher, much much much more.

house, clowns, chocolate painting, ice cream cook off, dunk hay ride and much much

Sunday, June 24ᵗʰ, 2012
At School
12:00 – 2:00 PM

Background options

Change the background color or add a picture

HOW TO DO IT

You can add effects to the background of your document.

1 From the **Page Layout** tab, select the **Page Color** button.

2 Select a background color.

3 To add effects or use a picture, select **Fill Effects** instead. The "Fill Effects" dialog box appears.

Remember!

Page backgrounds look great but are just for looking at on screen. They don't print out.

4 The "Gradient" effect changes the background color shades.

5 To have a picture as your background, click the **Picture** tab, click the **Select Picture...** button and choose a picture on your computer.

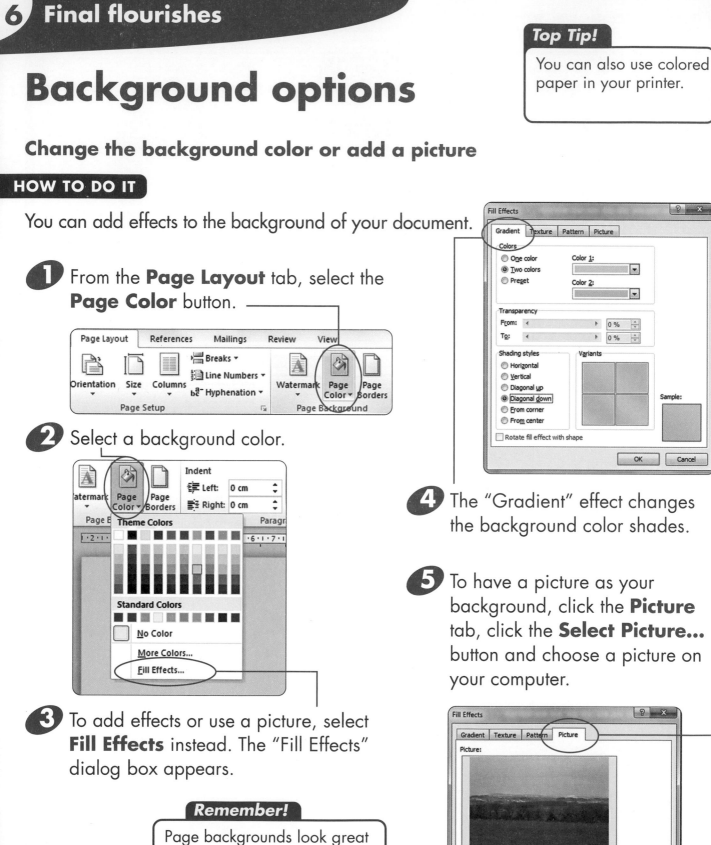

PROJECT 5 SCHOOL FAIR POSTER

A blue-shaded background will have an impact

It won't print, but looks great on screen!

1 Click the **Page Layout** tab and the **Page Color** button drop-down menu.

2 Bring up the "Fill Effects" dialog box and click the **Gradient** tab.

3 Create a "Two colors" gradient with two different light blues.

4 Select "From corner" in the "Shading styles" panel and select a variant. Click **OK**.

Fill Effects dialog box:

Gradient | Texture | Pattern | Picture

Colors
- One color
- Two colors
- Preset

Color 1:
Color 2:

Transparency
From:
To:

Shading styles
- Horizontal
- Vertical
- Diagonal up
- Diagonal down
- From corner
- From center

Theme Colors

Standard Colors

More Colors...

Rotate fill effect with shape

Sample:

OK | Cancel

Border patrol

Adding Borders to your pages

HOW TO DO IT

A good border improves the look of some documents.

Top Tip!

Many of the "Art" options are old-fashioned looking. Stick to the patterns.

1 Click the **Page Borders** button on the **Page Layout** tab. The "Borders and Shading" dialog box appears.

3 The "Art" drop-down menu lets you make fancy borders.

2 Set the "Page Border," "Style," "Color," and "Width" options. Check different effects in the "Preview" panel.

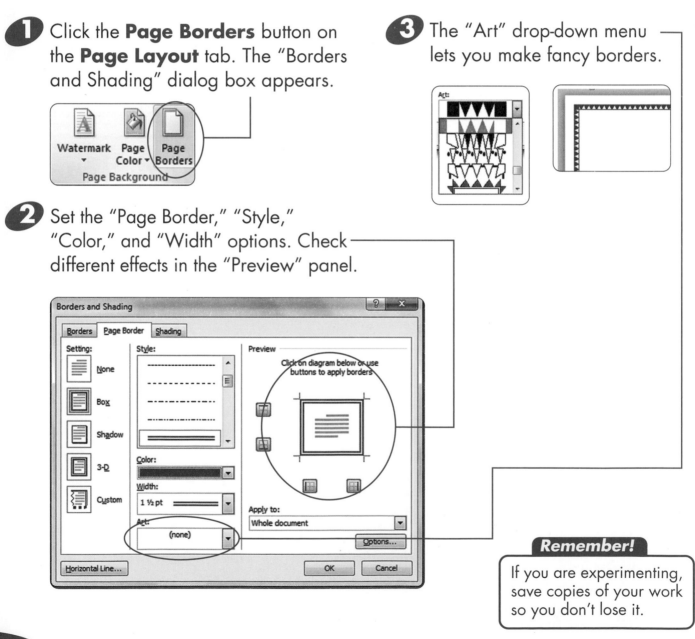

Remember!

If you are experimenting, save copies of your work so you don't lose it.

PROJECT 5 SCHOOL FAIR POSTER

A border – and it's done!

Absolutely the final touch

Adding a border frames the poster nicely.

 Click the **Page Borders** button and bring up the "Borders and Shading" dialog box.

 Add a border in a color that matches everything else.

 Try using an "Art" style.

 Save and print your poster.

Presentation options

Using the standard **Cover Pages**

HOW TO DO IT

Word comes with this option to help beginners make their work look good.

1 Open a new document. Click the **Cover Page** button on the **Insert** tab.

2 Select a Cover Page style.

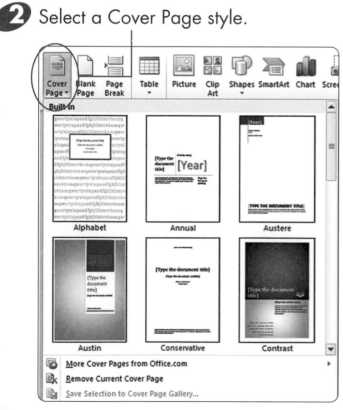

3 Type into the places indicated to complete your cover page.

PROJECT 6 PERSONAL PROFILE

Create a cover page for your profile

Use a standard cover page to start

Make sure your personal profile looks good immediately.

USING IT

1 Open a new document and save it as *Personal Profile*.

Mod

Challenge!

Cover pages are created using standard **Word** formatting. Click on each element to see how it's done.

2 Insert a standard cover page using the *Mod* style.

3 Fill in the fields with a title and other appropriate information.

Personal Profile
Howard Measle

Headers and footers

Remember!
Hover-over the tools in the **Design** tab for more information about them.

Link your pages together with standard text at the top or bottom

HOW TO DO IT

"Headers" and "Footers" help keep your document together.

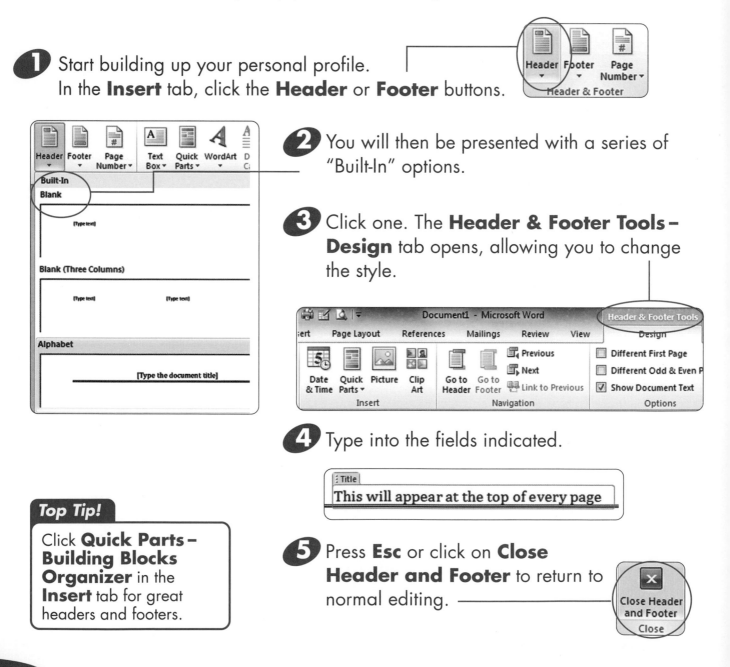

1 Start building up your personal profile.
In the **Insert** tab, click the **Header** or **Footer** buttons.

2 You will then be presented with a series of "Built-In" options.

3 Click one. The **Header & Footer Tools – Design** tab opens, allowing you to change the style.

4 Type into the fields indicated.

5 Press **Esc** or click on **Close Header and Footer** to return to normal editing.

Top Tip!

Click **Quick Parts – Building Blocks Organizer** in the **Insert** tab for great headers and footers.

PROJECT 6 PERSONAL PROFILE

Add headers and footers

Tie your pages together with headers

A title on every page will help people reading the document.

1 Start creating your profile content. Set the "Style Set" to *Distinctive* and use *Title* as your style. Create content for *Contents, Personal Details, Academic Achievements, Extra-Curricular Activities,* and *References.*

2 Click the Header button to add a header. Use *Mod* to tie it in with the cover.

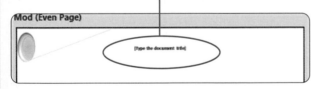

Mod (Even Page)

[Type the document title]

3 Notice that **Word** uses the title from the title on the cover. This is because the field names are the same.

Personal Profile

4 The *Mod* style has two versions, *Odd* and *Even.* Use the "Different Odd & Even Pages" option in the "Options" toolset to allow you to apply both versions.

☑ Different First Page
☑ Different Odd & Even Pages
☑ Show Document Text
Options

5 Add your name as a basic footer. Use the **Format Painter** to make the text look the same as the Header title.

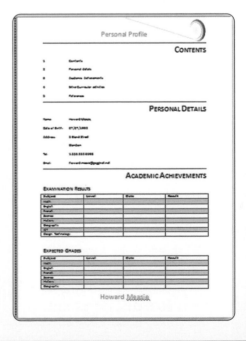

Page numbering

Page numbering helps keep your print-out in order

HOW TO DO IT

Page numbers help the reader know his or her position in a document.

 From the **Insert** tab, click the **Page Number** button drop-down menu.

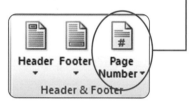

 Decide where the page number needs to go.

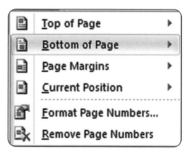

Top Tip!

You can create a "Table of Contents" including page numbers if your Header styles are consistent. See the **References** tab.

③ Select a page number style from the list available.

Page X of Y
Bold Numbers 1
Page 1 of 1
Bold Numbers 2
Page 1 of 1

④ Format the page numbers using the Font toolset, or if the number is in a Text Box, the **Drawing Tools – Design** tab.

Footer
Page 1 of 1

⑤ Close Headers and Footers to return to normal editing. Double-click on the header or footer to change it again.

PROJECT 6 PERSONAL PROFILE

Number your profile pages

Explore page numbering options

Add page numbering to complete your profile.

1 Click on your first content page and then click on **Page Number** in the **Insert** tab.

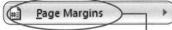

2 Select the **Page Margins** option and then "Accent Bar, Left."

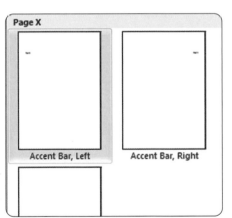

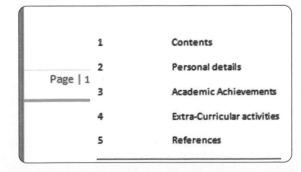

3 A number box appears at the top left of your page with the **Drawing Tools – Format** tab and the **Header & Footer Tools – Design** tab. Change the styling to make the numbering more distinct.

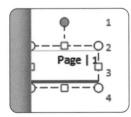

4 Because of the "Different Odd & Even Pages" option being set, you need to repeat this on the next even page.

5 Save and "Print Preview" your profile.

Time for a break

Remember!

The "Zoom slider" in **Print Preview** helps you see several pages at once.

Page and Section Breaks

HOW TO DO IT

Adding "Page Breaks" stops you worrying about pages shifting as you add text.

1 Move the insert point to where you want to start the new page.

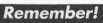

2 From the **Insert** tab, click the **Page Break** button.

> This paragraph should have the page to itself.
> This paragraph should be on the next page

> This paragraph should have the page to itself.

> This paragraph should be on the next page

3 If you want to change the layout between pages, you need to use "Section Breaks."

4 In the **Page Layout** tab, click the **Breaks** button drop-down menu.

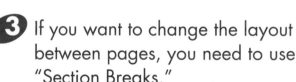

> This paragraph needs to be portrait
> This paragraph needs to be landscape

Top Tip!

The keyboard command for page break is **Ctrl** + **Enter**.

5 Select the **Next Page** option to allow you to change the orientation after the break.

> This paragraph needs to be portrait
>
> This paragraph needs to be landscape

6 If you have headers and footers, you need to click off **Link to Previous**

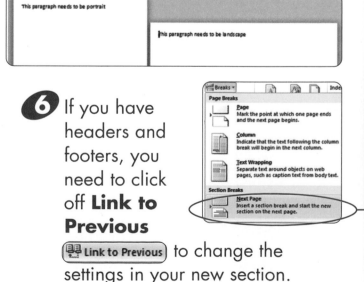

 to change the settings in your new section.

Split up your profile, using breaks

Breaks will split up your profile nicely

Each section of the profile should be on its own page.

1 Insert a page break at the beginning of the *Personal Details*.

2 Add a section break at the beginning of *Academic Achievements*.

3 Click on the Orientation button to change this section to landscape.

4 Add another section break before *Extra-Curricular Activities*. Make it portrait again.

Creating text columns

Remember!

Use small fonts to get lots of information on a page.

Lay your work out in columns

HOW TO DO IT

Text columns make reading easier. Newspapers use this styling.

1 Click where you want the columns to start.

2 If this is not at the beginning of a document, add a section break, otherwise the whole document will change into columns.

3 In the **Page Layout** tab, click the **Columns** button drop-down menu.

4 Click on a standard column format, or select **More Columns** to define your own.

Insert	Page Layout	References	Mailings

Margins Orientation Size Columns Breaks ▾ Line Numbers ▾ Hyphenation ▾

Page Setup

One
Two
Three
Left
Right
More Columns...

My document with columns

After a section break I now have three columns. After a section break I now have three columns. After a section break I now have three columns. After a section break I now have three columns. After a section break I now have three columns. After a section break I now have three columns. After a section break I now have three columns. After a section break I now have three columns.

After a section break I now have three columns. After a section break I now have three columns. After a section break I now have three columns. After a section break I now have three columns. After a section break I now have three columns. After a section break I now have three columns. After a section break I now have three columns. After a section break I now have three columns.

After a section break I now have three columns. After a section break I now have three columns. After a section break I now have three columns. After a section break I now have three columns. After a section break I now have three columns. After a section break I now have three columns. After a section break I now have three columns. After a section break I now have three columns.

Then another section break

5 Add another section break and select the **Columns** button drop-down menu to return the document to one column.

Top Tip!

Use the **Hyphenation** button to break up long words in your narrow columns.

Hyphenation ▾

PROJECT 6 PERSONAL PROFILE

Add columns to your profile

Use columns on a page with lots of text

If you are going to wax lyrical, break it down into columns!

1 Add a new heading, *Personal Statement*, after *Personal Details.*

> **Continuous**
> Insert a section break and start the new section on the same page.

Breaks ▾
Line Numbers ▾
Hyphenation ▾

Columns ▾

Watermark ▾
Page Color ▾
Page Borders

Inde

Page Background

2 Add a "Continuous" section break and then click on the **Columns** button. Select "Two."

One

Two

3 Write your personal statement. There is a section break after it already so you don't need to add another one.

PERSONAL DETAILS

Name: Howard Measie
Date of Birth: 07/07/1992
Address: 5 Bland Street
Blandon
Tel: 1.555.252.6598
Email: howard.measie@gogginet.net

PERSONAL STATEMENT

I am a conscientious student, who enjoys school and aims to get the most out of every opportunity afforded me. I have been very fortunate to find many areas and subjects in which I do well. With the support of the excellent teaching staff I believe I will achieve excellent results in my upcoming examinations in line with those that I achieved last year.

Outside school I have a full and active social life, which I never allowed to interfere with my academic achievements.

I am particularly proud of the progress I am making towards achieving my Black belt in Karate. I am not a natural athlete, so it as taken a lot of hard work. At my last Grading I achieved my first Grade 1 result after nearly 4 years of trying, so I am definitely improving.

I am passionately aware of environmental issues and follow my responsibilities as a consumer

Getting on edge

Setting Page Margins

HOW TO DO IT

Changing "Margins" helps your work fit onto a page.

1 "Margins" are set from the **Page Layout** tab or the **Print Settings**.

2 There are several standard schemes.

3 If these do not suit, select **Custom Margins**.

Custom Margins...

4 The "Page Setup" dialog box allows you to set the margins exactly.

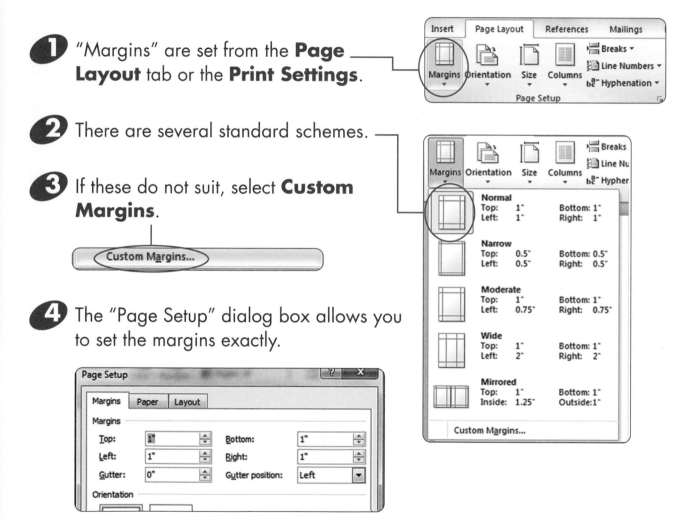

Make the most of your paper

Make your profile fit the page

Create your profile and set the margins accordingly.

1 Create a Custom Margin that is slightly wider than the "Normal" setting. Use this on your landscape sections.

2 Preview your work.

3 Click on your *Personal Statement*. Make the margins "Narrow."

4 The column section now has narrow margins while the rest of the page is normal. Change back, or make it match.

Adding comments

Make notes in your document as a reminder

HOW TO DO IT

"Comments" let other people know why you have done something on group projects.

 Select text you wish to add a "Comment" to.

 In the **Review** tab, click the **New Comment** button.

Top Tip!

For comments that <u>do</u> get printed out, use footnotes.

 A red marker and comment bubble appear. Type your comment into the bubble.

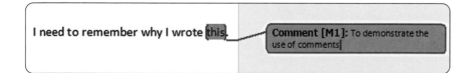

I need to remember why I wrote this. — Comment [M1]: To demonstrate the use of comments

 Use the **Delete** button to delete a selected comment, or all comments, on a document.

Delete
Delete All Comments Shown
Delete All Comments in Document

Remember!

You can also print your work and write on it.

Add comments to the profile

Use comments to remind you of your thought processes

USING IT

It could take several days to do a good job on the profile. Use comments to remind you what"s still outstanding.

1 Add a comment if you need to double-check your examination results.

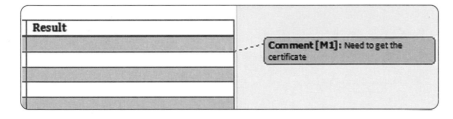

2 Remind yourself that you used a section break to allow you to use columns.

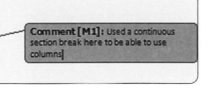

3 If you are sure you know how to do that, delete the comment.

4 "Print Preview" the document to check that the comments will not be printed.

Help is always there

Did we lose you on one of the projects?

Word has help built in. If you are connected to the internet there is more.

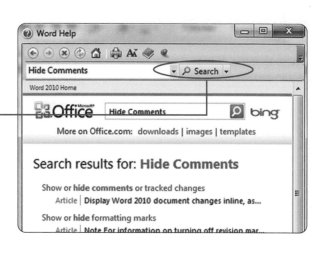

1 To get "Help," click the icon.

2 Type your question into the search field and click **Search**.

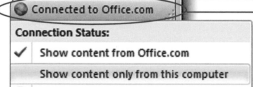

3 If you are on the internet, "Help" will show answers to your question, including videos.

4 If the connection is slow or not working, you can change the connection status manually by clicking on the button at the bottom of the pop-up.

5 If you are not connected, you will see only help that is built into the program.

PROJECT 7 USING THE HELP MENUS

Get yourself some help!

Some questions to explore

There are lots more tools to look at. Use **Help** to find out about them.

1 Search for help on the **SmartArt** button.

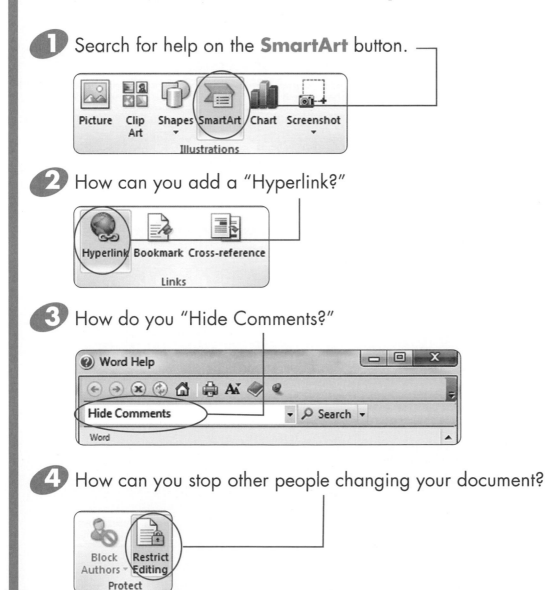

2 How can you add a "Hyperlink?"

3 How do you "Hide Comments?"

4 How can you stop other people changing your document?